# EXACT METHODS IN
# LINGUISTIC RESEARCH

# EXACT METHODS IN LINGUISTIC RESEARCH

O. S. Akhmanova • I. A. Mel'chuk
R. M. Frumkina • E. V. Paducheva

*Translated from the Russian by*
DAVID G. HAYS *and* DOLORES V. MOHR
The RAND Corporation

UNIVERSITY OF CALIFORNIA PRESS
BERKELEY AND LOS ANGELES    1963

# TRANSLATORS' PREFACE

Akhmanova's Preface explains why this book was published in the Soviet Union. All that remains is for us to explain why we have translated it.

Computational linguistics, or mathematical linguistics, is developing at least as rapidly in the United States as in the U.S.S.R. Here, too, it suffers the growing pains that Mel'chuk describes in Chapter IV. Linguists tend to frown a bit at the computer, to sneer somewhat at statistics and information theory; but perhaps they will be interested in reading the views of *linguists* who find statistics and even electronic computing machines useful. One purpose of the translation, therefore, is to make a *linguistic* introduction to the new field accessible to Western scholars.

Another purpose is to disseminate a rather full and probably accurate view of today's most influential Soviet work in computational linguistics. This survey no doubt represents the best work presently being done in this field in the U.S.S.R.; hence it is not a representative sample. On the other hand, the future of the field is sure to be influenced more by the substance, amount, and quality of the best, rather than the average, current work. A reasonable prediction, using that premise and the information in this book, is that computational linguistics in the U.S.S.R. will develop rapidly and produce a fair share of the world's knowledge in the field.

This book is, nevertheless, fairly weak in some respects. The linguist whose curiosity and interest are stimulated by the chapters on statistics and information theory should consult a statistician or mathematician at once, before attempting any applications himself. Better techniques are available, and more significant applications are possible. But Chapters V and VI are not offered as handbooks—as introductions, they may be more acceptable than would be mathematically sophisticated but linguistically naive treatments.

This translation was prepared in support of a continuing program of research in linguistics and machine translation undertaken for the United States Air Force by The RAND Corporation.

D. G. H.
D. V. M.

# PREFACE

The present book is an attempt to throw some light on several results attained by science in the area of the applications of exact methods to linguistic research. The concept of exact methods in science, and of exact sciences, is inseparably bound with mathematics—whence the expression "mathematical linguistics" to designate this new direction in linguistic research. It is hardly proper, however, to elevate this expression to the level of a technical term, since such a term could lead to a distorted conception of the nature of the question. The essence of this direction and its real content consist not of creating some special kind of "linguistics," but rather of perfecting, of making accurate, reliable, and modern, the methods of linguistic research in the usual meaning of the word. Thus, it is clear that the authors would prefer to eliminate the phrase "mathematical linguistics" from the title of the present book.[1] It is impossible, however, to ignore the fact that this term has already attained a certain popularity, and therefore it seems inexpedient to avoid it altogether.

The book has four sections,[2] dealing with the following topics:

(a) Those questions of general linguistics that must be clarified if the discussion of concrete methods of exact study and the description of linguistic phenomena, in the following chapters, are not to seem too far removed from earlier linguistics.

(b) The place and role of machine translation in contem-

---

[1] [We have done so.—Tr.]
[2] [Chapters I, II, III; IV; V; and VI.—Tr.]

porary linguistics in a theoretical-linguistic as well as in a practical sense.

(c) Possible applications of statistical methods to linguistic research, together with a discussion of the basic principles of statistical analysis and such basic statistical concepts as *random event, frequency,* and *evaluation of accuracy.*

(d) Possible applications of information theory to language study.

Nowhere in the present book have we treated linguistic applications of "nonquantitative" mathematics—in particular, mathematical logic. This large question requires separate study.

The amount of factual detail that has been developed in different areas of language study by exact methods is not uniform, and this fact has influenced the content of the corresponding sections of the book. Thus, in Chapter V, it has proved possible to discuss machine translation rather fully, not only presenting many of its theoretical and practical problems but also summarizing basic approaches to the solution of these problems. The same point applies in essence to Chapter VI as well, where we have presented a rather detailed analysis of studies dealing with the application of the methods of information theory in language study.

On the other hand, in describing the role of statistical methods in linguistic research, it has been more convenient to reduce the critical survey of the literature to a minimum and to concentrate on the basic concepts of statistics and the basic principles of statistical analysis. The reason for such an organization of the fifth chapter is that statistical methods have been applied in linguistics for a rather long time, and the literature in this field is so large and specialized that any thorough critical review of it would have led to an unjustifiably great enlargement of the book and a distinct disproportion in its parts. Chapters I and II were written by O. S. Akhmanova, Chapters III and IV by I. A. Mel'chuk, Chapter V by R. M. Frumkina, and Chapter VI by E. V. Paducheva.

O. Akhmanova

# CONTENTS

CHAPTER I

# Can Linguistics Become an Exact Science?

"Ever larger areas of science are undergoing a salutary infusion
of mathematics; an ever greater portion of the sciences is going
over into the ranks of the exact. One can foresee a swift development of this process in the decade ahead." (From an
article by Acad. A. N. Nesmeyanov, "A Look at the Tomorrow
of Our Science," *Pravda*, January 1, 1960.)

## 1. Linguistic "Content" and Linguistic "Expression"

High-speed electronic computers have given all areas of knowledge analytic means of astonishing capability. The "electronic
brain" makes possible the solution of problems formerly not
open to calculation.[1]

Among the basically new areas for the application of electronic computers, machine translation and automatic information retrieval occupy an important place. The first models of
machines for automatic translation from one language into another, and of information machines, which collect a huge store
of knowledge in their "memories" and put it out on demand in
any sequence of combinations, have already been created; these
machines have a truly great future.[2]

---

[1] Bibliographic references for Chapters I and II will be found at the end of
Chapter II; similarly, those for Chapters III and IV will be found at the end of
Chapter IV. The bibliographies for Chapters V and VI follow each of the chapters.

[2] Here is what Acad. A. N. Nesmeyanov says on this subject in the article

These two problems—machine translation and automatic information retrieval—are alike in that their solution demands a basically new approach to language, the development of specialized methods of research on, and description of, language. This new approach can be briefly defined in the following fashion. One must learn how to represent grammatical, lexical, lexico-phraseological, and other regularities of language in such a form that one can input them directly to the apparatus. In other words, it is necessary to "decode" the processes with which language communication is performed. Mathematics, with its inexhaustible possibilities, must provide the basis for a much deeper penetration into the "mechanism" of language and for a thoroughly strict and logical, fully "rational" description of the regularities it uncovers.

As is well known, language is the most important means of human communication; but, at the same time, it is the immediate activity of thought, the tool of development and struggle. Therefore, it is perfectly correct to approach language from different although closely interrelated directions. Concentrating on the communicative function of language, one quite rightly represents it primarily as a form of communication; hence, one can justifiably attempt to consider language merely as a vehicle, a structure for the transmission of previously prepared communications, and even simply as an indication of the existence of internal and external experience.

Language, however, is not just a vehicle for the transmission of prepared thoughts; it is the action of thought itself. Therefore, if language is a vehicle, it is one that not only facilitates mutual understanding but also helps regulate thought, organize experience, and develop social self-consciousness.

---

cited above: "The dream of information machines is not unfounded, especially if we recall that at present scientific knowledge—in the natural and technical sciences alone—is communicated throughout the world in tens of thousands of journals. Chemistry alone occupies more than ten thousand journals. Frequently, it is extremely difficult to find this or that fact at its hiding place in this ocean of scientific literature. I remember a statement by a scientific worker in an American firm to the effect that if a scientific task costs less than several hundred thousand dollars it is easier to redo it than to search for it in the literature.

"Scientific-information machines undoubtedly have a great future."

Only through the discovery of all facets of language can one achieve a full understanding of its nature as a unique social phenomenon. Language should be studied in connection with research on the causal bonds between linguistic communication and the facts of the social life of its creators and bearers, with their history, culture, and literature. There is not the least doubt that modern exact methods of research will soon permeate all areas of our science, and that linguistics, in the fullest and broadest sense of the word, will assume an entirely modern aspect. But for the present, when only the first steps are being taken in this new direction, a quite definite and deliberate restriction and confinement of the area of research is unavoidable. Concretely, as will become clear from the following outline and description of the present condition of science in the area under consideration, research is confined to two areas:

(a) limited and specific spheres of application of language, namely, the language of the exact sciences, especially mathematics;

(b) only the communicative ("intellectual") function, the description of problems of intellectual communication as abstracted from the emotional, aesthetic, volitional, and other aspects of language.

Limitation of research initially to the intellectual-communicative function of language seems to give one the right, for given specific purposes, to consider language as a particular kind of "code system," while the actual "products of speech," formed from the elements of a given "code" and bearing definite "information," may be considered to be "communications" that have a unique and precisely definable relation to this code system. But it proves to be an extremely difficult matter to apply this approach in practice. Ordinary human language is not a code such as necessarily presumes a one-to-one correspondence between a fully defined content and a definite expression. Hence, the most diverse difficulties and complications are inescapable.

In languages abounding in so-called synthetic forms, the absence of a simple one-to-one correspondence between the designator and that which is designated, or between expression and content, is most graphically evident. For example, in the Russian *em* [I eat], as in all nonproductive formations in general, it is impossible synchronically to separate out those parts of the designator, or expression, that would correspond to such designata, or contents, as (a) the concept of the process of eating, (b) indicative mood, (c) first person, (d) singular, (e) present tense. Nor can simple one-to-one correspondences be formulated for regular, or productive, formations, between the elements of such forms as, for example, *zval* [called], *bral* [took], *dal* [gave], and the various contents expressed by them—tense, person, number, voice, and mood, in conjunction with specified material meanings.

Considered theoretically, each of the separate meanings contained in compounded complexes similar to those just mentioned can be abstracted, or intellectually separated out, into a sort of "minimal unit of meaning," and it is quite natural to propose that those using language also intuitively perform analytic operations of a similar type. But if such operations are to be transferred from the area of intuition into the area of logic and rationality (and no machine can operate otherwise), a definite minimal unit of expression must be made to correspond regularly and sequentially to each minimal unit of meaning. As one can see from the examples cited above, however, in natural human language *several* minimal units of meaning often correspond to *one* minimal unit of expression. The picture is even more complex if one considers that very frequently one and the same minimal unit of meaning turns out to be embodied in several completely different minimal units of expression—a fact that is observable, for example, in the co-occurrence in language of various types of noun declensions, different ways of expressing the same categories of verbs, etc.

Thus far, we have used only two concepts—meaning (content) and expression; i.e., for the initial presentation of a problem it has more or less been taken for granted that we were dealing with just two aspects of linguistic units. But, in fact, linguistic research and description become possible only with a fully detailed and distinct delineation of "expression" as the external sound capsule of morphemes, on the one hand, and of the sounds in a language, considered as members or elements of its phonological system, on the other. For example, *t* or *l*, in such words as *plot* [raft], *zhaket* [jacket], *portret* [portrait], *bal* [ball, dance], *avral* [the command for "all hands on deck"], *fal* [lift—a part of a ship's rigging], on the one hand, and *berët* [takes], *nesët* [carries], *vedët* [carries], *zval* [called], *bral* [took], *upal* [fell], on the other, will be treated entirely differently by a language. In the first six words, these sounds are not to be separated out as minimal units of expression, corresponding to minimal units of content; i.e., they do not "morphologize." But in the second group, they emerge quite consistently and regularly as the outer wall of the sound capsules defined as "units of content."

Between these two basically different phenomena, there lies the following empirically established difference. The sounds in a language, as elements of its phonological system, lend themselves to comparatively easy enumeration. In any given language, the number of functionally distinct sound units (phonemes) is quite small (20 to 60).

It is an entirely different matter when certain sounds belong not simply to the category of "distinguishers" but to the category of concrete, "individually" fixed capsules of only these and no other morphemes (e.g., the *t* in *berët* [takes] or in *razbityj* [broken], the *u* in *nesu* [I carry] or in *bratu* [to a brother], the *a* in *zhena* [wife] or in *stola* [of the table] or in *doktora* [the doctors]). Here, it becomes extremely difficult to take an inventory of these morphemes, and their number is indefinitely great. Units of expression of this type, being "ambivalent," are immediately associated with units of content or meaning; and these latter units are correlated with reality, reflecting the multiplicity of these relations in which the most diverse phenomena are found.


*2. "Homoplanar" and "Heteroplanar" Approaches to the Treatment of the Question of "Sound" and "Meaning"*

From what has been said, it should be clear that clarifying the relation between the content (meaning) of linguistic units and their expression (especially their sound) is the main problem of contemporary linguistics. Therefore, it is natural that the "homoplanar," mechanical concept of descriptive linguistics and the "heteroplanar," immanent concept of glossematics have long been the objects of serious criticism from various points of view, including that of Soviet linguistics, particularly in relation to the treatment of the question of content and expression, explicit and implicit, that these systems accept. In insisting that linguistic study and description proceed without analysis of the meaning of the registered units (since this would demand a consideration of processes not reducible to "operationalistic" research), the proponents of descriptive linguistics seem to oppose not only the "psychological" and "logistic" tendencies of the nineteenth century but also contemporary neo-saussurianism, which postulates a double nature for linguistic signs, demands a heteroplanar approach to linguistic phenomena, and insists that the object of linguistics cannot be limited to a spoken and syntagmatic level alone but must necessarily include a paradigmatic level also. In one particular aspect of neosaussurianism—in glossematics (as distinguished from descriptive linguistics)—it would seem that the question of meaning as related to sound occupies an especially large area, and is, in fact, the basis of the whole theoretico-linguistic construction.

The foregoing situation apparently follows from the fact that the basic method of glossematics is that of "commutation," or the "commutation test," the application of which permits the discovery of an "invariant" of language, through determination of the correlation between the levels of expression and content. Actually, this does not hold. In glossematics, the levels of expression and content are not at all the same thing as sound and meaning in the usual and natural sense of these words. In the same way, the special glossematic disciplines—"kenematics" and "plerematics"—are not at all the same as phonetics and semasiology. It is basic for the two levels that together compose the semeiological invariant that they be functors (members) of a given function,[3] which is why the names "level of content" and "level of expression" have a conditional character. Besides, with regard to "kenemes" and "pleremes," glossematics carefully distinguishes between the "form" of expression and content, on the one hand, and their "substance," on the other. The latter—i.e., the substance of expression and of content—are

---

[3] In the terminology of Hjelmslev, the word "function" is used to mean relation [12].

fully determined by their form, and even exist only as a result of the form ("solely by its grace"—*udelukkende af dens naade*) and can never in any case be considered as having independent existence.

In fact, glossematics allows one to perform an experiment that includes comparison of different languages with the purpose of extracting that which they have in common, regardless of which languages are subjected to comparison. That which is in common is designated by the Danish term *mening*. But, again, *mening* does not mean the same ("meaning") as in normal usage; this can be seen from the fact that in English translation the Danish *mening* is not to be rendered by its etymological analog—i.e., by the word "meaning"—but by the word "purport"—"understood by," "bringing to mind": that which is brought to mind by the use of this or that unit of language—i.e., that which is contained in the "intent" of the speaker transmitting the linguistic communication.

The position that the certain something contained in that intent—the purport of what is said—is in itself amorphous and indefinite, and takes on clear definition only after the form of the content of this or that language organizes it—so much was already formulated by De Saussure ([9], p. 112 *et seq.*). In glossematics this position underwent further development, and assumed an important place.

A portion of the spectrum is usually cited as explanation of what has been said about substance and form. For example:

| Language | Spectrum | | | |
|---|---|---|---|---|
| English | green | blue | gray | brown |
| Welsh | *glas* | | *llwyd* | |
| Russian | *zelenyj* | *sinij* | *goluboj* | *seryj* | *korichnevyj* |

*Mening*, in this instance, is the section of the spectrum itself. It is understood, or contained, in the intent; it is the "purport" of the utterance. But an utterance can be realized only when language "throws its net" over amorphous "purport," and gives form to the amorphous substance of content—i.e., in this instance, arbitrarily splits it into two, four, five, or some other number of parts.[4]

The examples cited make it possible to elucidate the general concept of the relation between form and substance in content, on the one hand, and form and substance in expression, on the other, that we find in glossematics. But they do not help at all in explaining the relation between the substance of content and the substance of expression, i.e., between those parts of the entire structure that approach most closely the usual conception of meaning and sound. Moreover, it is easy to prove the absence of parallelism, the basic impossibility of a direct correlation of the two substances by the method of commutation, which, by the way, was most convincingly done by Siertsema[5] ([26], p. 149). As Siertsema has shown, a picture of the attempt to define the correlations would have the form shown in Figure 1.

It is entirely possible that all the extending bonds between linguistic research and the concepts and categories of mathematical (theoretical) logic will lead to a complete reorientation of the methods of glossematics and of its tests. Still, from

---

[4] In principle, the same should also be applied, as the result of a full symmetry of levels, to the relationship of form and substance in an expression, as in this example:

| Language | A cross section of the roof of the mouth, from lips to pharynx | | | |
|----------|:---:|:---:|:---:|:---:|
| English  | $p$ | $t$ | | $k$ |
| Lettish  | $p$ | $t$ | $k^1$ | $k^2$ |
| Eskimo   | $p$ | $t$ | $k^1$ | $k^2$ |

That is, if English $k$ includes the entire "palato-uvulo-velar zone," Lettish separates the velar and velopalatal, while Eskimo separates the uvular and velar.

[5] It is not without interest to note that in Siertsema's opinion this basic non-correlatability is the irrefutable proof of the basic inacceptability of the "method of commutation," which is the cornerstone of the whole glossematic structure.

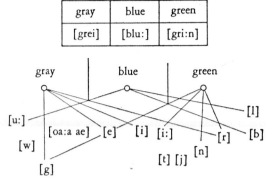

| gray | blue | green |
|------|------|-------|
| [grei] | [blu:] | [gri:n] |

FIGURE 1.   Result of an Attempt To Define Correlations
of Content and Expression.

the viewpoint of the special and concrete problems of linguistics, the following position remains, in fact, effective: Although descriptive linguistics departs from the homoplanar principle, and glossematics from the heteroplanar, in the treatment of the phenomena presented here, the factual understanding of the correlation of sound and meaning is (if one puts aside terminological differences and gets to the heart of the matter) the same in both these directions. Therefore, Hjelmslev's scheme—

| Linguistics | | | |
|------|------|------|------|
| The substance of content | The form of content | The form of expression | The substance of expression |

emerging from his definition of linguistics as a science in which the study of expression is not "phonetics," and in which the study of content is not "semantics"—fully corresponds to descriptive linguistics' postulated exclusion of phonetics as "*prelinguistic*," and to its exclusion of meaning from research. Much has been said and written about this. For both schools, the basic subject of linguistic science is the study of "structures"; reduction of these structures to two levels also appears, in fact, to be general for both—in essence, Hjelmslev's "unit of expression" and "unit of content" correspond exactly with the "phoneme" and "morpheme" of descriptive linguistics.[6]

### 3. A Compromise between the Homoplanar and Heteroplanar Approaches

As noted frequently in the literature, meaning, though in fact the basis of all descriptive morphology, has not received either official recognition or any definition in this linguistic school. Therefore, it is quite intriguing to come upon a treatment of this question of meaning in Gleason's book, *An Introduction to Descriptive Linguistics* [5] (especially since this book has been translated into Russian and has thus become widely known among Soviet linguists).

Gleason's solution to the question of sound and meaning is very interesting. Being above all a popularizer, Gleason imme-

---

[6] As is known, the publication in America of Hjelmslev's work, in English, has greatly facilitated closer relations between the two schools [12]. E. Haugen's review on this subject is very interesting (*IJAL*, Vol. 20, No. 3, July, 1954, pp. 247–251).

It seems especially easy to draw a parallel between Hjelmslev's "prolegomena" and Z. S. Harris' generalized monograph on descriptive linguistics [29]. Both Hjelmslev and Harris completely repudiate the concepts of morphology and syntax (Hjelmslev, p. 76 of the Danish edition; Harris, p. 262); they both develop methods for segmentation into "immediate constituents" on the basis of substitution (Hjelmslev, p. 38; Harris, p. 369); both tend toward a description distinguished by its maximal simplicity, exhaustive character, and consistency; both consider it their ultimate aim to structure texts of a given language (Hjelmslev, p. 16; Harris, p. 372), demanding that the researcher leave aside purely formal criteria, and placing relations at the center of attention, not the related objects—entities—as such (Hjelmslev, p. 22; Harris, p. 365); both construct a description at sequential levels, which together make up what Hjelmslev calls a "hierarchy." (A hierarchy is a class of classes, consisting of a series of segmentations from the largest to the smallest units that can be obtained through research. Each such class is similar to what in American linguistics is called a "level.")

The basic difference, which according to Hjelmslev is that research should begin with entire texts (in order to segment them subsequently on the basis of commutation), cannot be considered essential; in fact, it is entirely unimportant whether one begins with the largest or the smallest units, especially since in practice linguists usually begin "in the middle"—*in medias res*—using as "texts" such utterances as are easily reproduced within *substitution frames*.

diately ran into the complete impossibility of a comprehensive and consistent presentation of the question of meaning, and its relation to sound, in the terminology of descriptive linguistics. But the terminology of glossematics seemed too abstract to be presented without change as a basis for the concrete methods of description that compose the main part of the book. For this reason, he took the terminology of glossematics, but gave it, in addition, a much simpler and more commonly acceptable meaning. The result: "Linguistics is the science which attempts to understand language from the point of view of its internal structure" (see p. 2). To penetrate the structure of language, one must bear in mind the fact that "language operates with two kinds of material. One of these is sound. . . . The other is ideas, social situations, meanings—English lacks any really acceptable term to cover the whole range—the facts or fantasies about man's existence, the things man reacts to and tries to convey to his fellows. These two, insofar as they concern linguists, may conveniently be labeled *expression* and *content*" (see p. 2).

It turns out that language, from the nature of the "two levels" that create it, is represented by two constituents—content and expression. Consequently, it is pointless to insist on the necessity of developing methods that would allow the study of language without resort to meaning, and one of the basic theoretical postulates of descriptive linguistics is completely refuted. For Gleason, too, the basic subject of linguistics remains "the internal structure of language," but it must not be studied by "purely formal methods, with no regard to meaning."

As has often seemed to be the case, this basic postulate of descriptive linguistics was justifiable by the basic impossibility for the linguist scientifically to define meaning. Definitions of meanings should occupy all the other sciences, which study not words and their combination in speech, but objects (e.g., only an astronomer can define the meaning of the word "moon"). The possibilities for a scientific description of meaning, and, in general, a solution to this question from "mechanistic" ("operational") positions, are not now proposed; nevertheless, although the nature of content in language remains undetermined as before (something for which there is no suitable word but which, in general, includes various things such as "ideas, social situations, meanings . . ."; see above), now, it is not so far removed, and it constitutes a part of language along with expression.

From the above exposition, it is clear that although Gleason uses the terminology of glossematics, he applies it arbitrarily: For him, content and expression are, respectively, what Hjelmslev calls the *substance* of content and the *substance* of expression. The structure of expression may be obtained by research on the series of sounds regularly recurring and subject to prediction. As for the structure of content, although the idea of a strictly parallel structure on both levels is preserved here as well, a much less clear explanation is forthcoming. "The speaker includes what he says within the limits of an organizing structure. This structure forces him to choose several features for description, and determines the means by which he *interrelates* them. It also analyzes the situation in a particular fashion. These *selected features,* like the above-mentioned sounds, also form *patterns which recur,* partially predictable. These recurring patterns are the structure of content."

It seemed useful to pursue somewhat further the corresponding sections of Gleason's textbook, since they very clearly reflect the unsatisfactory condition that obtains in the study of one of the basic (if not *the* basic) questions of linguistics, and in the two most important directions of linguistic structuralism. Gleason's textbook is quite typical in this respect, since the author did not take into account a criticism of the "descriptive" and "glossematic" concepts—a criticism at once very serious and convincing, and having a more and more definite and categorical nature.


### 4. "Primary" and "Secondary" Segmentation in Language

Among those works which, in criticizing the extremeness of descriptive linguistics and glossematics, compare constructive doctrines to the doctrines of the former, an article by A. Martinet, "Linguistic Arbitrariness and Double Articulation" [18], is especially interesting for a study of the question of sound and meaning (*les sons et le sens*); this article gives the results of the previous criticism of the concept of isomorphism [2]. By insisting on the absolute parallelism of the two levels—content and expression—glossematics (and after it, descriptive linguistics as well) gives a distorted picture of the actual state of affairs. Even leaving aside the excesses of the transcendental doctrine that regards content and expression as only the "functors of the sign function," and turning from Gleason's generally available interpretation, the main points will still be overlooked: (1) the hierarchy of meaning and sound, the subordination of the second to the first, the leading role of the first in relation to the second,[7] and (2) the necessity arising therefrom for a much finer analysis of the subject—an analysis that shows most convincingly that the question is in no way reducible to two sides (*faces*) of a linguistic "sign."[8] There cannot be the least doubt that the basic opposition is an opposition of phonemes, on the one hand, and the designator-designated, on the other. In schematic form, this relationship (if we turn to the example shown in Figure 1) will appear as given in the table below.

---

[7] ". . . *la subordination des sons au sens qui semble incompatible avec le parallelisme intégral que postule la théorie*" (he has in mind the theory of isomorphism); A. Martinet [7], p. 105.

Usually (normally), meaning is so leading and determining in the communicative functioning of linguistic units that those using a language do not notice the many properties of the level of expression—the sound material of language. The latter emerges at the former level and takes on independent meaning only in special cases, such as onomatopoeia (*Lautmalerei*), proper names, etc. O. S. Akhmanova has devoted an article in the jubilee collection for Acad. Petrovici to the specific role of "sound" in proper names.

[8] As R. O. Jakobson [14] has most convincingly shown, the inherent tendency of some representatives of neosaussurianism to join up whatever you please within the framework of the "designator-designated" dichotomy is the fruit of a misunderstanding. This is not De Saussure's innovation but simply a repetition of a theme 2,000 years old. Definition of the sign (*signe*) as a *juncture* of designator and designated coincides literally with the *semeion* of the Stoics, composed of a *semeinon* and a *semeinomenon,* and with the adaptation of the ancient Greek model of St. Augustine in the form *signum = signans + signatum.* One should add (and this has become especially obvious since the publication of R. Godel's work [11]) that, as frequently happens to posthumous publications that did not receive the author's approval, something emerged in the form of a finished (and original) concept which, to the author, was only a stage in the yet incomplete development of a direction of research.

| 1st Segmentation[a] (*première articulation*) Bilateral Units (morphemes and words) | | 2nd Segmentation[a] (*deuxième articulation*) Unilateral Units (phonemes) |
| --- | --- | --- |
| [blu:] as a whole, as a global, unsegmentable unit, unitarily and directly related to meaning, having a definite semantics | [blue], corresponding to a certain part of the spectrum, etc. | differentiating the sound capsule of a given morpheme from all other morphemes [b] [l] [u:]. The basic property of these units is that they are not immediately correlatable with meaning. |

[a] In Martinet's terminology, the first segmentation yields a minimal bilateral unit (the morpheme of the majority of structuralists), and the second yields sequential and minimal unilateral units, of which the basic function is a differentiation (phonemes).

In other words (a reality clearly not reflected in the abstraction of the glossematic scheme) there are, on the one hand, distinguished ("opposed") phonemes and, on the other hand, designators and designata, "objects" (in the broad meaning) and words—bilateral units, basically different from phonemes, which are the unilateral units of the "differential level."[9]

Of course, when we say words (and not morphemes), we deliberately break with the established tradition of contemporary linguistics, since morphemes, as ultimate units of the first segmentation (or "semantic level"), must theoretically be the basis of the whole consideration. However, if we simplify the discussion on the theoretical level, the preference of morpheme to word artificially simplifies and schematicizes the facts. But the basic problem of contemporary linguistics is precisely to free

---

[9] The question of the relation of primary and secondary segmentation received very interesting treatment in A. Martinet's well-known studies in historical phonology [7]. Although the author of this article disagrees with A. Martinet's basic tenets (including the role of the system in change in the sound relations, the concept of the principle of "economy," the role of sound properties which are not "differential," etc.—see L. Zgusta's review on this subject in *Archiv Orientalni*, Vol. 27, 1959, pp. 338–341), the system of contemporary phonological concepts is presented in this book so clearly, and the contemporary problematics of "secondary segmentation" is developed so fully, that the value of this book to the science of "sound languages" can hardly be overestimated.

itself from schemes and dogmas and to turn to a study of the contemporary problems of human communication in all their real complexity and uniqueness. The ultimate units of real communication are the minimal components of sentences—words. And words have complex meanings, composed of different elements and segmentable at various levels and in various aspects. For example:

(1) *"Categorical" Meaning.* A word's belonging to one "word class" or another (for us, the parts of speech) provides it with a categorical semantic capsule (a general or "categorical" meaning, belonging to an entire given class or series of words), with which is encapsulated a particular, individual part of the semantics of a word—its "semantic nucleus." Therefore, for example, the Russian *gorod,* compared with the French *ville* and the English "town," will yield the picture shown in Figure 2.

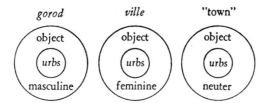

FIGURE 2.   Categorical (Semantic) Capsules.

The "categorical (semantic) capsule" of a word is tied in, on the one hand, with general rules for its combination with other words (its grammatic requirements) and, on the other hand, with its individual lexical nucleus and its own special meaning content. Therefore, one or another categorical semantic capsule of a word may more or less closely adjoin its individual nucleus, or it may, on the contrary, be easily separable from the latter: In some cases, what is contained as one aspect in the nucleus is simply emphasized—e.g., the aspect of substantivity in the semantics of the word *gorod;* in other instances, the categorical semantic capsule can add to the semantic nucleus a certain aspect not inherent in it as such—e.g., the aspect of "substantivity" in the semantics of a deverbative noun.

(2) *Meaning Derived from Component Morphemes.* Corre-

sponding with the morphological structure of the base of a word, in its general semantics, we can more or less distinctly separate out the meanings of individual word-forming morphemes entering into its composition, i.e., such morphemes as the roots and lexical (word-forming) affixes. The meaning of an individual morpheme within the composition of a word may be only very distantly and obliquely connected with its general lexical semantics, and not only not help in its discovery but even hinder it, such as in the Russian *otrada* [joy, delight] (why *ot* [from, of]? [*rada* = joy]); in *gromootvod* [lightning rod—lit., thunder conductor] (which does not carry off thunder); in the German *Walfisch* (whale-fish, although a whale is not a fish), etc.[10]

The selection and classification of "elementary meanings," with the purpose of subsequently rendering them by nonlinguistic symbols on some large scale, presupposes the solution (if only in working form) of a number of problems of general semantics that we shall discuss below. But this solution remains as yet undiscovered. Furthermore, up to the present, even the method of approach to these problems is unclear. On the one hand, we have every reason to believe that "pure meaning" is, in general, nonexistent, and that there exists only the meaning bound up with language; every language already bears its own particular variant of cumulative meanings, its own complex image of reality. On the other hand, a directly contrary approach is still postulated with great insistence. It is insisted that the direct analysis of languages, predominant at present, must unavoidably end in failure, just as a physicist would prove helpless if he tried from the beginning to apply his own laws to natural objects—trees, rocks, etc. The physicist starts by relating his laws to the simplest constructions—to an ideal lever, mathematical pendulums, point masses, etc. Armed only with laws relating to these constructions, he later finds himself able to analyze the complex behavior of real bodies, and thus to regulate them.

---

[10] For a more detailed treatment of this question, see [3], p. 43 *et seq.*, and [1]. A special work by A. I. Smirnitsky [8] is devoted to a detailed consideration of the question of sound and meaning from the point of view of the semantic structure of a word.

As we shall show later, the basic problems of general semantics were in the past subjected to calculation and proof by practice with concrete problems in the composition of subsidiary international languages. Now, these problems take on new meaning and special relevance in connection with the problem of so-called machine language, about which a few words may be said here.[11]

The problem of an artificial language (machine language) as a general language for computational linguistics emerges in two forms: in the area of machine translation, in the form of an interlingua [intermediary language—Tr.];[12] and in the area of machine information retrieval [search of literature—Tr.], in the form of an information language. The distinction between an interlingua and an information language lies in the fact that the first has as its goal the translation into a single system of the entire content of those languages among which it "mediates," to become a generalized net of relations, having no right to discard or drop any single item of the content that exists within the languages bound by it. Therefore, one can accept a definition of it in terms of a "recoding" of natural languages, and regularly study different languages as only an alternation of the code (*one language is a codified form of another*). As distinct from an interlingua, the language of the information machine is free to simplify or to complicate its structure as desired, arbitrarily to select and combine "elementary meanings." Therefore, the question of an information language touches on the basic problems of language structure in general, questions of its modeling and rationalization—and has great significance for general linguistics.

In working out machine languages, as in classic interlinguis-

---

[11] One should note that there already exist several projects on artificial languages: See, for example, the *Semantic Code Dictionary* of J. Perry, A. Kent, and J. L. Melton [22]; further, R. Ranganathan, "Natural, Classificatory, and Machine Languages," in *Information Retrieval and Machine Translation* (A. Kent, ed., Interscience Publishers, New York, 1961, Part 2, pp. 1029–1037); Bolting's "Steniglott" in the *Proceedings of the Cleveland Conference for Standards on a Common Language for Machine Searching* (September 6–12, 1959); the "Descriptors" of Mooers (C. N. Mooers, "Zatocoding Applied to Mechanical Organization of Knowledge," *American Documentation*, Vol. 2, 1951, pp. 20–32); *et al.*

[12] See Chapter IV, Sec. 5.

tics, "autonomists" and "naturalists" (see [4], p. 47) are clearly distinguishable. Bolting's *Steniglott* gives 4,000 words for Greek, Latin, English, German, and Slavic languages. The most concrete application of the naturalist principle to the creation of an information language is found in J. Perry and A. Kent; the semantic multiplier for a class of machines will be MACH; for a class of crystals, CRIS; for a class of documents, DOCM; for a class of diffusions, DIFF; for a class of gases, GASS; for a class of minerals, MINR; for a class of metals, METL; etc.

# CHAPTER II

# The Place of Semantics in Modern Linguistics

## 1. Linguistic Meaning and Translation

As was shown in the preceding chapter, a basically new approach to the question of meaning is urgently necessary for the development of modern methods in linguistic research. Although this new approach has only recently appeared before researchers in its fullest form, many different efforts to develop it have occupied "interlinguists" of various tendencies for a long time. Many of these efforts not only have not yet lost their significance but, on the contrary, have now taken on special meaning in connection with the basically new problems mentioned above—various forms of modeling and rationalization of linguistic communication, which, by the way, are closely bound with new content inserted in the concept of translation. In contemporary linguistics, translation is not unjustifiably defined as one of the basic problems of human communication: One or another form of "translation" necessarily presupposes not only the study of a foreign language and the mastery of one's own, but also mastery of every expression and communication of thought and of experience. It is quite obvious that the central problem in translation (and, consequently, in contemporary linguistics in general) is the question of meaning.[1] Therefore,

---

[1] On the problem of meaning as a basic problem in MT, see Chapter IV.

this question now appears at the center of the linguist's attention.

This extremely broad concept of the essence of translation lies at the basis of the concept of meaning as a purely semeiotic fact; from this point of view, both for linguists and for all who use languages naturally, the meaning of a linguistic "sign"—concretely speaking, "word"—is nothing else but the *translation* of it by means of another sign, usually one more fully developed. Translation is of three kinds: (1) intralingual, i.e., the explanation of verbal signs by means of other signs in the same language; (2) interlingual, i.e., properly speaking, the translation or explanation of verbal signs in one language by means of verbal signs in another language; and (3) intersemeiotic translation, or *transmutation,* which means the explanation of verbal signs by means of *nonverbal* sign systems [15]. The most widespread and up to now the most important form of translation in practice, i.e., interlingual translation, usually presupposes not the exchange of individual signs in one language for individual signs in another, as "code units," but rather the replacement of whole statements in one language by equivalent statements in the other, i.e., equivalence in difference. This latter is the basic problem of language and the main subject of linguistics. Without a solution to this problem, neither a description of languages nor the creation of dictionaries and bilingual grammars is possible.

All that is available to knowledge can be expressed in any existing language; hence, the absence of grammatical correspondence can be supplemented by lexical means. It is more difficult to replace missing special expressions, terms, and words. Since languages are distinguishable for the most part not by what they *can* express but rather by what they *must* express, repeated translation of a message between two languages tends to impoverish it. However, the fuller the context, the less will be the loss of information.

The ability to speak in a certain language includes an ability to speak about that language; a conscious (or intellectual) level of language permits and even requires interpretation by an exchange of code, or by translation. Therefore on the conscious or intellectual level there can be no discussion of untranslatability. But in mythology, magic formulas, poetry, etc., the picture changes basically. Here is involved not only translation in its essential meaning but also creative transposition, which can take three forms: (1) intralingual transposition from one poetic form to another; (2) interlingual transposition from one language to another; and (3) intersemeiotic transposition from one symbolic system to another, i.e., from the sphere of the artistic word to music, dance, cinematography, or painting.

This new and very interesting approach to translation as a new and perhaps key problem of linguistics in general, i.e., a clear and productive classification of the various aspects of translation (especially productive in promoting the development of automatic translation, where the problem of intersemeiotic translation takes on a special meaning), deserves the most serious attention. However, its general methodological premises demand serious discussion. From the standpoint of the most general foundations for corresponding structures, the whole multiplicity of studies can be reduced to two basic approaches: (1) studies proceeding from an understanding of meaning as a semeiotic fact in the sense developed above; (2) studies proceeding from the fact that "understanding" a word or group of words, and consequently "accepting" them in general, and then "transmitting" the linguistic communication are possible only when there exists some conception of an "intralinguistic" object, designated by a given linguistic unit, or a conception of the phenomenon of objective activity. Therefore, the meaning of a word cannot be reduced to translation or to "metalinguistic definition."

The meaning of a word is a reflection of an object, a phenomenon, or a relation in conception (or a mental formation, analogous in character, constructed from reflections of the individual elements of the activity); it enters the structure of a word as its so-called internal aspect; with respect to which the sound of a word emerges as the material shell necessary not only for the expression of meaning and for its communication to other people but also for its appearance, formulation, existence, and development. Therefore, if, for example, a person blind from birth has never seen chalk, milk, snow, or any other white object in general, then the meaning of the word "white" will never become fully manifest to him. The normal speaker has never seen centaurs or unicorns, but he is not at all surprised that they are defined in every language by the same words as a horse is, because in his extralinguistic experience he has had revealed to him the attributes of the real animal and so does not need a particularly extravagant flight of fancy in order to transfer them to imaginary beings. The meaning of a word used in a particular native language to designate objects as completely distinct—from the point of view of Central European culture— as "egg," "deceased," and "bread" is manifest only to one who has acquired an extralinguistic familiarity with these objects in a given cultural area, and who has seen an oval form ascribed not only to bread but also to the bodies of the dead at burial, etc.[2]

It follows from the above that translation is the language-receiver's creation of a natural equivalent to a message, natural because nearest in both meaning and style. In order to attain the most complete communication possible, one needs not only a high degree of mastery of the linguistic structures involved but also a deep penetration into the differences between the cultures being compared. Hence, the concept of an "ethnolinguistic structure of communication." Therefore, the problem of comparing meanings in various languages grows more complex as the possibility of deriving the comparison from nonverbal stimuli decreases—i.e., from nonlinguistic situations, and as the compared languages differ more from each other with respect to their culture and history. Under these conditions, it becomes highly complicated to correlate meanings in the languages, which are being compared by means of the extralinguistic situation and by derivation of the meaningful parts of a communication.[3]

---

[2] It is thought that the examples introduced by R. Jakobson in the article cited in Chapter I deal with the same matter; in order to translate into English *prinesi syru i tvorogu* as "bring cheese and cottage cheese," the translator has to refer to the object, to extralinguistic reality; he must imagine what certain objects (phenomena, relations, etc.) are called in the life of a particular people, or what he can most conveniently and comprehensibly call them if such objects are unknown to a particular people or are uncommon in its everyday life.

[3] See Willard Quine [24], pp. 153–154. For example, a rabbit runs by and a native says "*gavagai*"; on the level of "empirical" meaning there is every reason to correlate this "*gavagai*" with "rabbit" or "There's a rabbit." But should there be a "terminological" correspondence between *gavagai* and "(There's) a

Unlike the "ethnolinguistic," the "properly linguistic" or "microlinguistic" structure of a communication stands out most sharply in the distinctions of word classifications (the noncoincidence of word-classes and of the generalized meanings connected with them), which are distinctions in the systems of grammatical categories, especially on the level of noncoincidence of necessary grammatical information.[4] But the main difficulty lies in the different relationship of abstract and concrete words (i.e., the differences in the semantic structure of words), the noncoincidence of their grammatical spheres, the specifics of the phraseological bonds, the different relations of linguistic form and semantic function, and so on. All of these and similar questions urgently demand the quickest possible solution, since without it further development of our science is impossible.

## 2. The Question of Linguistic Meaning and the Search for Semantic Universality

The definition of meaning (of words) cited above is based on a delimitation of the internal side of language as a specific linguistic category of the concept that apparently comprises the category of logic.

However, it does not follow from what has been said that logical categories in general should not occupy the linguist, or that he should remain indifferent to the question regarding the nature of conception. On the contrary, it is extremely impor-

---

rabbit"? That is, does the utterance in the native language mean the same as "rabbit" does in English; or does *gavagai* refer, unlike "rabbit," to any small quadruped or, on the contrary, only to a particular species of rabbit, requiring a lengthy description to designate it in English? These are questions to which our attention is called constantly and repetitiously in general semeiology (Whorf and Sapir give interesting materials from a comparison of English and North American Indian languages).

[4] For this reason, the translation of verse 13, chapter 4, of the Gospel according to St. Matthew into Villa Alta, for example, turned out to be difficult; in this particular dialect of the Zapotec language (Southern Mexico), the opposition of completed versus repeated action is a grammatic necessity, so that it is impossible to know whether Christ visited Capernaum *before* the event described there [19].

tant to explain the relation of meaning and concept. But not nearly enough has been done as yet in this area. Therefore, the problem now remains of explaining the relationship between meaning and concept in particular (scientific concept), which textbooks on logic apparently attempt to do; one textbook defines *concept* as "an idea about an object which defines its essential characteristics" (V. F. Asmus, *Logika* [Logic], p. 33[5]). Until this is done, it will remain unclear what relationship this higher concept has toward words and their meanings, i.e., toward the objectively existing units of various languages as actually spoken. Indeed, natural human thought cannot exist without language, linguistic terms, and phrases; apparently, this also remains true for thoughts that define an object's essential characteristics.[6] It is here, in fact, that the coöperation of spe-

---

[5] *Logika*, Gospolitizdat, Moscow, 1947.

[6] In treating these questions, it may be useful to distinguish the "meaning" of a word from its "sense," which is what A. I. Smirnitsky does in his above-mentioned, as yet unpublished work: "The meaning of a word quite frequently seems to be not monolithic but structurally complex and therefore to distinguish components in its own make-up that might not correspond to any object attributes that are separate in the sense of the word, or that might correspond to them only approximately or conditionally. In other words, the meaning of a word might have a complex composition and a definite structure that may or may not, entirely or exactly, be aspects of the word's sense, i.e., aspects of the theoretical or practical concept expressed by the word. Thus, in the word *gromootvod* [lightning rod, lit., thunder conductor] the components *grom(o)-* and *-otvod* are clearly distinguishable; consequently, the meaning of *grom-* somehow enters into the composition of its semantics, although this semantic component does not exist in the sense of this word, since a *gromootvod* is generally understood to be an apparatus for "leading off" not thunder but an electrical charge—lightning. The semantic component *grom* does not enter into the structure of the concept; although the latter is practical and is expressed on a general scale by the word *gromootvod*, still it exists in the general semantics of the word.

"The semantic formation of a word can sometimes be tolerated by a language for a long time (i.e., by the society speaking a given language) in a particular form, even when it is essentially divergent from the word's sense, if the word can be construed as a kind of conditionality, or as a joke, etc. But in some well-known cases, depending on various concrete circumstances, the contradiction between the semantic formation of a word and its sense leads to a change, or to the substitution of another word not containing such a contradiction. In contemporary literature, the name *gromootvod* is more and more frequently being replaced by the word *molnieotvod* [lit., lightning conductor], which

cialists in various disciplines—linguistics, mathematics, philosophy (logic), psychology, etc.—is extremely important. Much attention has recently been turned to such coöperation. However, in seeking new and more complete means of answering these questions it is necessary, as we have already said above, to consider the experience of previous work, primarily of the "interlinguists," i.e., of those scientists who, from various positions and by varying methods, sought possibilities for the creation of a rationally constructed, logical, and convenient international auxiliary language.[7]

As we know, in many areas of human communication there have long existed international semeiotic systems recognized by everyone: The international telegraph code, the international metric system of weights and measures, musical notation, mathematical symbolism, etc. The work in progress on standardization of terminology in various areas of science and technology is constantly pursuing this goal.[8]

In spite of the success already achieved, however, many questions connected with the principles of the formation and function of auxiliary languages still remain arguable and incompletely answered. From this fact there emerges a lack of unity and coördination of effort that is harmful to the development of international communication through the medium of an auxiliary language. As is generally true of questions of translation, these questions have a general-linguistics character; one might say that a survey of the main questions regarding the formulation of auxiliary languages is essentially the same as a survey of the most crucial problems of linguistics in general.

Rationalization of communication through auxiliary interna-

---

describes the matter more accurately. The relationship between the semantic formation of a word and its sense is, as we know, historically variable; it changes primarily in relation to the development of the sense, conditioned by the development of a society and its new encounters with various aspects of life, and also in relation to the aspects of a language's internal development—with changes in its phonology, grammatical structure, and vocabulary."

[7] For a short treatment of the history and contemporary status of the question of an international auxiliary language, see [4].

[8] As we know, this work was begun thirty years ago by the International Federation of National Associations for the Determination of Standards; the Academy of Sciences of the U.S.S.R., through its projects on technical nomenclature, took a large part in this work (for materials, see [13]).

tional media in the areas enumerated above was easily attainable because of the complete determinability and autonomy of the designata. Thus, for example, a meter is 1/40,000,000th of the Earth's meridian; a centimeter is 1/100th of a meter, and a millimeter is 1/1,000th. The integral sign $\int$ is a symbol representing the limit of a sum; $\prod^n_{i=1}$ is a symbol that represents the product of $n$ terms; "dot-dash," or a group consisting of one short and one long impulse, is a simple conditional equivalent of the letter $a$, regardless of its position in a word or of what the word or group of words means, or even of whether the word means anything at all (the Morse alphabet can transmit with equal success real words and phrases with real meaning or meaningless collections of letters). International standardization of terminology is based on exact definition of the designated objects, and without such a basis it would be impossible and meaningless. Difficulties arise in the standardization of specialized terminology whenever a choice has to be made among various terms present in different languages; here, we run into questions of national preference, word-formation possibilities, and relations with other terms. But still, however difficult it may be to decide whether, for example, to call a certain substance "gasoline" (English), *"essence"* (French), *"Benzin"* (German), or even something else, this is not the basic or most important difficulty. The "designatum," its nature, and its properties are quite precisely and "autonomously" definable.[9] Whichever word one may choose to designate a particular object, a precise and monolithic definition of that object itself must necessarily precede such a choice.

Furthermore, to apply this principle in formulating an international auxiliary language that would purport to aid communication among the peoples of diverse and distant regions, we need definitions of the most widely divergent designata, and a complete listing and classification of them, and at the same time definitions of designata in the broadest possible sense—not just objects, actions, and attributes, but various con-

---

[9] In this connection, it is interesting to note that all these words, like many modern technical terms in general, are incidentally "artificial" or "contrived" words, for which reason a choice of one of them would not be forced by reference to the "fundamental" or "natural" elements of language.

tents of relations: direction, cause, independence, and other complex logical and psychological categories. Such attempts have been made and are constantly being made.[10] One can see how great a value is attached to this question from the multiplicity of different "semantic" theories.[11] However, most research in the latter direction has an abstract, philosophical character, and very little to do with the physical, linguistic side of the question, or with the factual peculiarities of human communication through language. In their attempt to regulate human communication, researchers often take a sharply a-prioristic position, based on abstract rationalistic structures and not on studies of fact. They do not study the possible ways to regulate it semantically according to the principle of the preservation of mutual understandings already arrived at within natural, historically developed limits.

In the present publication it is neither possible nor necessary to consider in detail the condition of general semantics, or the possibility in principle of a complete inventory of all the "designata" known to modern, developed languages in the form of "universals," autonomous with respect to these languages. This question is mentioned here only insofar as it seemed necessary to state, on the one hand, that the linguistic specialists and creators of auxiliary international languages (who, as we know, were for the most part not linguists) are aware of the primary importance of general-linguistics research and, on the other hand, that the existing auxiliary international languages were set up (developed) without any fundamental, preparatory in-

---

[10] As an example, one may refer to the system of forty-five correlative words worked out for systematic expression of the basic differences between the concepts of quality, motive, time, place, means, possession, the quantity of an object, and its individualization. Note particularly, as a sample of especially deep and intense analysis, the semantic research of E. Sapir performed for the International Auxiliary Language Association—"Totality" [27] and "Grading" [28].

[11] By these we mean the various forms of general semantics associated with the philosophical semantics of Morris and Carnap and, on a more general level, with the logical positivism of Russell and Whitehead. A very clear exposition of the bases of "general semantics" is presented in A. Korzybsky's book *Science and Sanity* [16]. In many respects, Korzybsky's ideas correspond with the position of the "science of symbolism" of Ogden and Richards, formulated before 1928 [20].

ventory of semantic categories, which is why the work of their authors, unlike that of the international terminological commissions, could not be built on the principle of a search for the most convenient and effective means of designating some quite distinct, previously defined content. As we know, this basic problem of general semantics—i.e., the problem of separating out, inventorying, and classifying all the meanings and connotations inherent in human languages—is at present not only unsolved but is not even being studied broadly and intensively enough to obtain a clear perspective of its solution.

Naturally, such a state of affairs in the area of general semantics (as the term is used here) not only continues to hinder work on the formulation and perfection of auxiliary international languages but also is the reason for the insufficiencies and inconsistencies inherent in them.

In order to consolidate our remarks about the complexity of the designatum-designator relation in language, which causes difficulties in the development of a rational auxiliary means of international communication, we shall present several examples.

The methods recommended by A. Martinet in his well-known article [17] for choosing roots for an international European auxiliary language can be illustrated in the choice of a word for the concept *bashmak* [shoe] for *la notion de soulier*. But what is *la notion de soulier* (conditionally translated above as the concept *bashmak*)? The Russian word, *bashmak*, stands both for footwear and for a technical contrivance (like the English "shoe"), but in French, such a technical contrivance would be called not *soulier* but *sabot*. Unlike Russian, English and German use their [ʃu] even more broadly—e.g., the English "snowshoes," varieties of *lyzha* [skis, snowshoes]. And the German word for *perchatka* [glove] is *Handschuh* [lit., hand-shoe]. On the other hand, the basic Russian word for this concept is *obuv'* [footwear]: *u neë mnogo obuvi* [she has many shoes (of various kinds) ]; *v etom magazine prodaëtsya obuv'* [they sell shoes in this shop]; *obuvnoj magazin* [shoeshop], etc., while in English and German, for example, although such generalized expressions as "footwear," *Schuhwerk*, etc., theoretically exist, their use is in fact so limited and specialized that for an Englishman the natural "concept" will be "shoes," or *Schuhe,* etc., rather than the more collective equivalent of the Russian *obuv'* —"footwear," *Schuhwerk,* etc.

One basic and quite properly separate principle in formulating an auxiliary international language is economy of words— they should be so chosen as not to hide the individual "conceptual areas," but rather to give all the strictly necessary meanings, and to teach users how to do without semantic differentiations that are not strictly necessary for normal communication. But realization of this very proper principle, and actual application of it, force one at every step to deal with the question of what is *really* necessary. Which semantic distinctions are really superfluous or inessential? Is it essential or inessential, for example, in speaking about *ruka* [hand, arm], to distinguish between and differentiate its two parts (*main* [hand] and *bras* [arm])? And if this is not essential, then is it worth while to distinguish, for example, *plecho* [shoulder]? Why not simply call the whole member by one word and teach everyone to think "economically" about the corresponding object (or group of objects united under one name)? Is it necessary, in the auxiliary language, to distinguish motions directed *toward* from motions directed *away from* the speaker; are distinctions of the type "go-come" (or, correspondingly, *gehen-kommen* or *aller-venir*) essential from the standpoint of economy and choice? Russian gets along with the one word *idti.* We [Russians—Tr.] do not feel uncomfortable when we say *idi syuda* [come here] and *idi tuda* [go there]; but for an Englishman or Frenchman it would be meaningless to say "go here" or *vas ici.*

One question concerning the internal form of the designator is closely related to the problems just described, i.e., the question of what internal structuring is most convenient. Thus, for example, the concept *dom* [home, house] (*le concept de maison,* Martinet, *op. cit.,* same page) on the general-semantics level is sufficiently clearly defined as such from the point of view of the modern conception of European houses. But *dom* is simultaneously "building," "habitation," and "shelter," or "refuge," etc. Apparently, definite cultural-historical causes forced the ancient Germans, for example, to refuse any variants of the root *dem/dom* as expression of this particular concept—

a root not only known in ancient German languages but preserved in the modern (compare, for example, German *Zimmer* [room, chamber] and English "timber," etc.). There is hardly any doubt that in choosing the most proper of existent "semantemes" for the auxiliary international language, it is not sufficient merely to avoid misunderstandings and accidental (homonymic) correspondences; careful research in their semantics is also necessary from the standpoint of their internal structure and of their adaptability to the most adequate and perfect expression of the corresponding concepts.

These aspects can be illustrated most graphically by examples of lexical morphology (the morphology of word-formation). One can hardly doubt that it is most essential to the auxiliary international language that the greatest possible number of words entering into it be "motivated," that they have a transparent structure and a rationally constructed relationship between designator and designatum; furthermore, the combination of morphemes composing them must be monovalent and reversible.[12] But even this completely clear and rational general rule, this correct general principle, is far from simple to realize in practice. Indeed, why not construct the entire system of qualitative adjectives on an antonymic basis? Let each semanteme designate a given quality in its "positive" manifestation, and let the *absence* of this quality, or the presence of the opposite quality, be designated by means of a single, caritive prefix. This is done, for example, in Esperanto: *facila*—easy, *mal/facila*—difficult; *nova*—new, *mal/nova*—old; *antau*—before, *mal/antau*—after; etc. As has already been entirely correctly indicated in the literature,[13] in practice such a system often leads to obscurity and doubt, especially if we note that *mal* is well

---

[12] Thus, for example, if solution of all the complex problems dealing with the selection of a morpheme from among *tud-, worg-,* or *erg-, org-, labor-,* etc., leads to the choice of *labor-,* then *labor/ist* should mean worker, *labor/ist/ar/o,* workers in general; *labor/em/a* should mean industrious, inclined toward hard work; *labor/ist/al/a* would be the adjective for working; and *anti/labor/ist/al/a* would have the corresponding opposite meaning. At the same time, the complex structure obtained should be just as easily and sequentially subjectable to the reverse process of expansion to the same identical parts as were used in the synthesis.

[13] For example, see [13].

known to be a Romance prefix having a pejorative, not just caritive, meaning. In this context, we cannot fail to note yet another question: Is there always an actual, real preference in usage for a complex or clear, morphologically sequential, and regularly productive word, as compared with a simple word? For example, *ochki* [eyeglasses] is called *okulvitroj* in Esperanto, *binoklo* in Ido, *oculvitres* in Occidental, *lunetes* in Novial, and *perspecillos* in Interlingua. Of course, if, abstractly speaking, the analytic definition of *ochki* as eyeglasses has some particular preference, then, in fact, in real-language usage the connection of this concept with that sound, fixedly adapted in practice in language communication, may be much more effective, eliciting a conception of the corresponding object much more quickly and immediately. Therefore, if *binoklo*, for example, entered various languages and took on a positive "international" character in the existing natural languages, then would it not be simplest to introduce it into the auxiliary language (of course, reserving the right for each language using it to form any complex and productive words as needed, on the basis of the principle of morphological monovalence and reversibility)?

As we have already seen in the above example with the prefix *mal-*, it is often difficult to attribute to lexical affixes the abstract character necessary for monovalent and reversible word-formation. For this reason, the great interest that the composers of auxiliary international languages show in the phenomenon of conversion is quite natural, since conversion is a widely distributed method of word-formation in which the individual morphemes, or productive affixes, alone do not serve as the word-forming materials—rather, the word's paradigm does. It would seem that, unlike productive affixes, the paradigm, or system of grammatic affixes, has the advantage of allowing one to define in communication such fully clear and definite meanings as verbality, substantivity, attribution, etc. But, actually, even here the formulator of an auxiliary international language runs into great difficulty. In the first place, what does it mean to translate a certain root and another paradigm when, for instance, it is necessary to obtain a verb-meaning from a substantive root? In English, for example, "to shop" (and, correspondingly, (he) shops, shopped, shopping, etc.) means "to go into a shop to make a purchase"; yet, for example, "to ship" (ships, shipped, shipping, etc.) hardly means "to go after something on a ship," but "to convey by ship"; "to paper" (where "paper" means *bumaga*) primarily means "to put up wallpaper with glue" [*obkleivat' oboyami*] (although *oboi* is not in general just paper, but a particular kind—wallpaper); "to chain" in English means "to bind with a chain," while the French verb *chaîner* means "to measure with a chain" (*mesurer avec la chaîne*). In English, the verb "to feather," formed by a conversion from the noun-root "feather" [*pero*] means "to line with feathers" (with reference to birds' nests, and used transitively), while the German *federn* has three meanings, different from that of the corresponding English verb. Of course, there are correspondences among various languages; e.g., English "crown," "to crown," French *couronne, couronner,* and German *Krone, kronen* are quite sufficiently alike in the morphological-semantic respect. But word-formation in the auxiliary international language must be monovalent and reversible. It must be entirely ideal and cannot tolerate idiomatic surprises. For this reason, conversion does not help much in solving the problem. Nor can the question of general-meaning affixes (i.e., general verb-affixes, general noun-affixes, etc.) be considered entirely clear. We can illustrate the complexity of this question with an example from Ido, for which there was originally proposed the application of the suffix *-if* for the meaning "to produce," "to divide out"; *-ig* for "to do," "to make," "to transform"; *-iz* for "to accumulate," "to guarantee"; and *-ag* for "to use as an instrument." Since a practical application of this rule turned out to be very difficult, because of the necessity of solving in every instance various problems of a syntactic-semantic nature, such as the transitivity or intransitivity of verbs, an attempt was made to substitute the single verbal suffix *-i* for all these various suffixes; however, this, too, failed to attain wide distribution. For this reason, further work in this area continues to be carried out for case after case, without any real results being obtained that might lead toward a fundamental solution of these general problems.

# BIBLIOGRAPHY FOR CHAPTERS I AND II

1.  Akhmanova, O. S., "Eshche k voprosu o slove kak osnovnoj edinitse yazyka" ["More on the Question of Words as Basic Language Units"], *Vestnik Moskovskogo gosudarstvennogo universiteta,* Vol. 10, No. 1, 1955, pp. 83–93.

2.  ———, "O ponyatii 'izomorfizma' lingvisticheskikh kategorij" ["The Concept of 'Isomorphism' of Linguistic Categories"], *Voprosy yazykoznaniya,* Vol. 4, No. 3, 1955, pp. 82–95.

3.  ———, *Ocherki po obshchej i russkoj leksikologii* [*Notes on General and Russian Lexicology*], Uchpedgiz, Moscow, 1957.

4.  ———, and E. A. Bokarev, "Mezhdunarodnyj vspomogatel'nyj yazyk kak lingvisticheskaya problema" ["International Auxiliary Language as a Linguistic Problem"], *Voprosy yazykoznaniya,* Vol. 5, No. 6, 1956, pp. 65–78.

5.  Gleason, H. A., *Vvedenie v deskriptivnuyu lingvistiku* [*An Introduction to Descriptive Linguistics,* Henry Holt & Co., Inc., New York, 1956], Izd-vo inostr. lit., Moscow, 1959.

6.  Gutenmakher, L. I., *Elektronnye informatsionno-logicheskie mashiny* [*Electronic Logico-Information Machines*], Izd-vo Akademii nauk SSSR, Moscow, 1960.

7.  Martinet, A., *Printsip ekonomii v foneticheskikh izmeneniyakh* [*Économie des changements phonétiques; traité de phonologie diachronique,* Francke, Berne, 1955], Izd-vo inostr. lit., Moscow, 1960.

8.  Smirnitsky, A. I., "O zvuchanii i znachenii v yazyke" ["Phonation of the Word and Its Semantics"], *Voprosy yazykoznaniya,* No. 5, 1960, pp. 112–116. (Translated: JPRS 6588, U.S. Joint Publications Research Service, New York, January 17, 1961, pp. 65–74.)

9.  Saussure, F. de, *Kurs obshchej lingvistiki* [*Cours de linguistique générale,* Payot, Paris, 1916, 1931, 1949], Sotsekgiz, Moscow, 1933.

10. Uspensky, V. A., "K probleme postroeniya mashinnogo yazyka dlya informatsionnoj mashiny" ["The Problem of Constructing a Machine Language for Information Machines"], *Problemy kibernetiki,* Vol. 2, 1959, pp. 39–50.

11. Godel, R., *Les sources manuscrites du cours de linguistique générale, de F. de Saussure,* S. Dorz, Geneva, 1957, 282 pp.

12. Hjelmslev, L., *Prolegomena to a Theory of Language* (translated by Francis J. Whitfield), University of Wisconsin Press, Madison, Wisconsin, 1961, and Baltimore, 1953.

13. Jacob, H., *Planned Auxiliary Language,* Dennis Dobson, Ltd., London, 1947, 160 pp.
14. Jakobson, R. O., "Linguistic Glosses to Goldstein's 'Wortbegriff,' " *Journal of Individual Psychology,* Vol. 15, No. 1, 1959, pp. 62–65.
15. ——, "On Linguistic Aspects of Translation," in R. A. Brower, ed., *On Translation,* Harvard University Press, Cambridge, Massachusetts, 1959, pp. 232–239.
16. Korzybsky, A., *Science and Sanity,* International non-Aristotelian Library Publishing Company, Lakeville, Connecticut, 1948.
17. Martinet, A., "La linguistique et les langues artificielles," *Word,* Vol. 2, No. 1, 1946, pp. 37–47.
18. ——, "Arbitraire linguistique et double articulation," *Cahiers F. de Saussure,* No. 15, 1957, pp. 105–116.
19. Nida, E. A., "Principles of Translation as Exemplified by Bible Translating," in R. A. Brower, ed., *On Translation,* Harvard University Press, Cambridge, Massachusetts, 1959, pp. 11–31.
20. Ogden, C. K., and I. A. Richards, *The Meaning of Meaning,* K. Paul, Trench, Trubner & Co., Ltd., London, 1936, and Harcourt, Brace & Co., Inc., New York, 1930.
21. Perry, J., A. Kent, and M. M. Berry, *Machine Literature Searching,* Interscience Publishers, Inc., New York–London, 1956.
22. Perry, J., A. Kent, and J. L. Melton, *Tools for Machine Literature Searching: Semantic Code Dictionary; Applications; Equipment,* Interscience Publishers, Inc., New York, 1958.
23. Osgood, C. E., and T. A. Sebeok, eds., *Psycholinguistics: A Survey of Theory and Research Problems* (Social Science Research Council, Committee on Linguistics and Psychology —Report of Summer Seminar), Waverly Press, Baltimore, Maryland, 1954.
24. Quine, W. V., "Meaning and Translation," in R. A. Brower, ed., *On Translation,* Harvard University Press, Cambridge, Massachusetts, 1959, pp. 148–172.
25. Ramakrishna, B. S., and R. Subramanian, "Relative Efficiency of English and German Languages for Communication of Semantic Content," in *IRE Transactions on Information Theory,* Vol. IT-4, No. 3, September, 1958, pp. 127–129.
26. Siertsema, B. A., *A Study of Glossematics; Critical Survey of Its Fundamental Concepts,* M. Nijhoff, s'-Gravenhage, The Netherlands, 1955, 240 pp.

27. Sapir, E., *Totality* (Language Monographs published by the Linguistic Society of America), No. 6, Baltimore, Maryland, 1930.

28. ———, "Grading. A Study of Semantics," *Philosophy of Science,* Vol. 11, No. 2, 1944, pp. 93–116.

29. Harris, Z. S., *Methods in Structural Linguistics,* University of Chicago Press, Chicago, Illinois, 1951.

# CHAPTER III

# *Several Types of Linguistic Meanings*

It is clear from the preceding exposition that one of the most important problems confronting linguists is the explanation of what types or varieties of meanings exist in language, and how to distinguish them and separate them from one another. But it is hardly possible to deal further with questions of semantics without perfecting the corresponding metalanguage. As the first step, we shall deal with the question of so-called grammatic, syntactic, and lexical meanings, and in this regard we shall try to define such widely used terms as "grammar," "syntax," and "morphology," although we do not claim to have the last word in defining these concepts.

Everything expressed in language represents the level of content, or the sum, of linguistic meanings. Linguistic meanings ("designations"), from the standpoint of just what is being expressed, are of two types:

(1) Where the designations are definable as relations among linguistic elements (such as morphemes, words, and sentences), i.e., where some linguistic elements serve as symbols of relations among other linguistic elements, we shall speak of *syntactic* meanings.

(2) In all other cases, i.e., where the designations are not linguistic relations but rather something outside of language, or where they are some particular facts of reality (objects, ac-

tions, properties, abstract concepts, representations, etc.), or a relation of utterance to actuality, i.e., where linguistic elements serve as symbols of something extralinguistic, we shall speak of *lexical* meanings.

The concept of syntactic and nonsyntactic indicators (and, correspondingly, of meanings) can be defined more concretely as follows: Indicators are considered syntactic when they are used only in syntactic analysis of a text, i.e., when they are necessary only in order to find a governor for each word; all other indicators are considered to be nonsyntactic.

We shall note further that the name "lexical" is temporary for all nonsyntactic meanings; it will suffice until we can find a better term. One could call nonsyntactic meanings referential, and then further distinguish lexical and some other types of meanings among them. But this is a matter for further study.

Lexical and syntactic meanings must be expressed in all languages (see E. Sapir, *Language,* 1921). This means that in no language is an utterance without meaning if it consists of elements expressing both lexical and syntactic meanings. Here such meanings are necessarily expressed in general, and not specifically as being of one or the other type. In other words, language as a symbolic system demands the expression of both lexical and syntactic meanings in every utterance, but it is irrelevant for language in general (and in individual languages) just what meanings are expressed; this is determined by the content of an utterance, i.e., by extralinguistic factors.

Linguistic meanings (designations) are distinguishable from yet another standpoint. It may be the case that in one language several quite concrete[1] meanings (perhaps both lexical and syntactic) must be expressed, but not so in another language.

The concrete meanings necessarily expressed in a given language can be called the *grammatical* meanings of that language. Meanings not necessarily or individually expressed in a given language may be called the nongrammatical meanings of that language.

The statement that "grammatical meanings in a given language must be expressed in that language" has the following

---

[1] Here, and in what follows, the word "concrete" is used in the sense of "particular," "given," "just exactly this."

significance. For this purpose, meanings have a variety of indicators, one of which must appear in any utterance in which there is an element present whose meaning can be joined (semantically) with a particular grammatical meaning. Thus, in some languages a word of a particular class cannot be used without indicators having corresponding grammatical meanings. Among these indicators there may be a zero; in that case the physical absence of an indicator is understood to be just such a zero indicator. Thus, in English, the meaning of *number* is grammatical, and every noun must be accompanied by an indicator of number (zero—singular; -*s*—plural). In Chinese, the meaning of number is nongrammatical; therefore, although a noun may be accompanied by a number indicator (*yíge* and other enumeratives for the singular, *men* for the plural), this is not necessary. The absence of an indicator is not taken to be a zero-th indicator, and if in the Chinese noun the number indicator is physically absent, then the meaning of number for this noun remains unexpressed.[2]

The question of whether a meaning is grammatical often leads to a question about the presence of a zero indicator among the indicators of that meaning.

In other words, some designators (indicators) are optional from the standpoint of a language system: Their use is determined by extralinguistic factors (content) and their absence is not discounted as being a zero indicator. Other designators are necessary from the point of view of the language itself: Their use is determined by the language's structure and their absence is considered to be an indicator. Nongrammatical indicators correspond to the first type, grammatical to the second.

In practice it is not always easy to differentiate between optional and necessary indicators (i.e., to determine the presence of a zero among the indicators of a given meaning), because there are many transitional cases. For each concrete meaning (and, correspondingly, for its indicators), special study is needed. However, this problem lies beyond the scope of the

---

[2] "In Chinese, as in Japanese, any noun can be used with reference both to a real singular and to a real plural of an object; in other words, it does not formally contain a specification of number within itself." (A. I. Ivanov, E. D. Polivanov, *Grammatika sovremennogo kitajskogo yazyka* [*A Grammar of Modern Chinese*], 1930, pp. 218–219.)

present chapter; for our purposes it is sufficient to believe that we are able in some way or another to distinguish the grammatical meanings in a language from the nongrammatical.

Grammatical meanings can be both lexical and syntactic. For example, noun-number meaning in Russian is lexical (the distinction of nouns by number is conditioned by extralinguistic distinctions) and grammatical (since noun number must be expressed in Russian). Likewise, the meanings of gender, number, and case are, for Russian adjectives, grammatical and also syntactic (gender-number-case distinctions in adjectives are not connected with any extralinguistic distinctions but merely reflect the syntactic bonds of the adjective).

These grammatical meanings define the specifics of a language. The general arsenal of linguistic meanings (i.e., what can be expressed in a language) is about the same for all languages. And languages differ primarily in that one language "prefers" certain meanings and makes them obligatory, i.e., grammaticizes them, while another language does this with other meanings. There may be languages that do not have grammatical—i.e., concrete, obligatory—meanings; this was true of ancient Chinese.

The relation of the grammatical, on the one hand, and the syntactic and lexical, on the other, can be schematized as in Table 1.

TABLE 1

| Meanings<br><br>Attributes | Nongrammatical | | Grammatical | |
|---|---|---|---|---|
| | Lexical | Syntactic | Lexical | Syntactic |
| 1. Must this attribute be expressed? | − | − | + | + |
| 2. Are the expressed relations intralingual? | − | + | − | + |

In this regard, language theory can be divided into lexicology, syntax, and grammar. Lexicology deals with the expression of extralinguistic factors, whereas syntax has to do with the expression of all possible relations among linguistic elements. Grammar occupies an intermediate position between lexicology and syntax; it deals with both lexical and syntactic meanings, but only with those which must be expressed in a certain language (i.e., grammatical meanings).

The term "grammar" is applied here in a narrower sense than the generally accepted one; usually, grammar is understood to be not only the study of grammatical meanings but also the study of the relations among language elements—syntax. In order to avoid ambiguity and contradiction of the generally accepted terminology, the word "grammar" will be applied in the usual, traditional sense, and the study of grammatical meanings will be called "grammar proper."

All that has been said up to now is related only to the character of linguistic meanings as independent of the means of expressing them. Now we shall turn to these means, which are of two types, depending on whether meanings are expressed by them within the word or not:

(1) *Morphological,* i.e., means for the expression of any necessary linguistic meanings within the word. We identify affixing, alternation, reduplication, incorporation, for example, as morphological means.

(2) *Nonmorphological,* i.e., means for the expression of meanings outside the word. Here we identify the use of auxiliary words, word-order, etc.

(The quite complex question of word boundaries is not considered here; for the purposes of the present study it is sufficient to suppose that we can somehow define word-boundaries. Specifically, we consider—as in machine translation—a word to be a group of letters between two spaces.)

The difference between morphological and nonmorphological means is schematized in Table 2.

TABLE 2

| Attribute \ Means | Morphological | Nonmorphological |
|---|:---:|:---:|
| Do the given means express some meaning within the word? | + | — |

As we have seen, the terms "lexical," "syntactic," and "grammatical" are set apart by two attributes and characterize meanings independent of the means of expression. These terms refer to the level of content.

The terms "morphological" and "nonmorphological" are set apart by a single attribute and characterize a means of expression independent of the expressed meanings. These terms relate to the level of expression.

The first and second oppositions lie on different planes. For this reason, the generally accepted subdivision of linguistic theory into lexicology, morphology, and syntax is not valid from a terminological standpoint. Even if we disregard the definitions proposed above, in traditional usage morphology is ordinarily understood to mean the study of the forms of words, i.e., of the means of expression by word-formation (within the word), while lexicology and syntax are the studies of the corresponding meanings. The use of the word "morphology" in place of "grammar" can be explained by the fact that in those languages from whose study the terminology of modern linguistics was formulated (especially the Indo-European languages), grammatical meanings are expressed mainly by morphological means, and, conversely, morphological means are preferred in these languages for expression of properly grammatical meanings. Hence the confusion of the terms "morphology" and "grammar" (or, more precisely, "grammar proper"), the terminologically inexact expression "morphological category," and other difficulties.

Consequently, it is necessary to produce a distinction between the types of meanings (lexical and syntactic, grammatical and nongrammatical) and the types of expression of meanings (by morphological and nonmorphological[3] means). Using this plan of opposition, one can classify the facts of language; here there are eight groups:

(1) Morphological expression of grammatical lexical meanings, e.g., indicators of number in the nouns of French, English, Russian, and other languages.

(2) Morphological expression of grammatical syntactic

---

[3] Nonmorphological means are frequently called "analytic" and sometimes even "syntactic."

meanings, e.g., indicators of gender, number, and case in Russian adjectives; indicators of gender and number in French adjectives.

(3) Morphological expression of nongrammatical lexical meanings. Here the incorporation of lexemes in polysynthetic languages, word-compounding (German, Hungarian, and other languages), and also various instances of word-formation in Indo-European, Finno-Ugric, Semitic, and other languages are illustrative. A clear example of morphological expression of nongrammatical lexical meanings is the change in gender of the Arabic verb or suffixing of pronouns.

(4) Morphological expression of nongrammatical syntactic meanings, e.g., the slit-writing of prepositions with a noun in Arabic (*bi, li,* etc.); slit-writing of the copula *-a* with the nominal part of a sentence in Georgian; the inclusion of indicators in a verb for all its noun modifiers and conditions in Chinook.

(5) Nonmorphological expression of grammatical lexical meanings, e.g., articles and compound tenses in French, English, and German, or indicators—again separate words—of plural number, such as *rnams* and *dag* in Tibetan.

(6) Nonmorphological expression of grammatical syntactic meanings, e.g., the particle *to* before an infinitive in English.

(7) Nonmorphological expression of nongrammatical lexical meanings. This group includes the most diverse, quite ordinary cases: Lexical meanings are expressed by individual words—lexemes.

It may seem that if some lexical meanings are expressed by each separate word, then they are expressed within the word itself, and one should speak of morphological means. But this is not the case. We shall explain here, and elsewhere in this book, what is meant by an expression of meaning within a word. Take the word *dver'* [door]; this word expresses several meanings. Now, let us join to the meanings expressed by this word the lexical meaning of *otkrytost'* [openness] (i.e., the door is open). To do this, we must use another word (*otkryta* [open, is open]), not just some indicator within the first word (which we would use if we had to add the meaning of plurality—*dveri* [doors]). Therefore, we speak of nonmorphological means of expressing the nongrammatical lexical meanings with individual words—lexemes.

(8) Nonmorphological expression of nongrammatical syntactic meanings—conjunctions, prepositions, copulas.

As stated above, we do not claim the distinctions and definitions introduced to be final ones. They merely serve as an illustration of how one may work to make linguistic terminology more exact and to create a system of exact concepts without which the applications of new, precise methods to the study of language are greatly hindered and sometimes become impossible.

Precise terminology is important for all areas of linguistics and especially for machine translation, about which more will be said in the next chapter.

# CHAPTER IV

# Machine Translation and Linguistics

## 1. General Remarks

Machine translation is a new and fast-developing area of linguistics in which exact methods of research are widely applied; indeed, they are necessary for progress.

An ineluctable part of the work in machine translation (MT) is the description of linguistic facts but in a unique form—namely, as rules for transforming a text in one language into an equivalent text in another.

These descriptions, consisting of the iteration of necessary operations, are so exactly drawn up that they can be "accepted" and used by an electronic computer. Thus, the immediate basic factor occupying our attention is the description of languages by exact methods, which can be verified experimentally by MT.

To avoid occupying ourselves with the complex theoretical question of the existence of a scientific description, we can stipulate that the construction of working models is a highly effective technique for creating and verifying a description of any system whatsoever. We shall explain just what this means.

Let us assume that we are considering a group of arbitrary objects generated by a mechanism unknown to us. This mechanism is not available for immediate observation, and we can draw conclusions about it only from the results of its activity, i.e., from the properties of the set of objects that it has generated. Here we are interested in the particular mechanism only in a strictly defined sense: It is important for us to know just those aspects of its functioning that cause it to generate the particular set. None of the concrete properties of the mechanism or of its functioning are relevant to us.

By analyzing the totality of objects available to us from the mechanism, we can create a hypothetical description of it. To verify this description, we can construct a model of the mechanism based on it. This would be only a model and not a copy of the mechanism, since very many concrete properties of the mechanism will not have been studied, and in some respects the model will not resemble the mechanism itself at all. But if this model in function can generate exactly the same objects as the mechanism studied, then we can conclude that our model is adequate in the relevant respects and consequently that our description is accurate. (Of course, this description does not have to be unique; other equally correct descriptions are possible.)

A model for a generative mechanism such as that in our example is directly relevant to linguistics. Actually, the aim of linguistics is the description of language, i.e., of the system generating speech. The system itself—language—is not manifest to the researcher; he must deal only with the results of its functioning—with speech. To verify one's descriptions, one can create working models corresponding to them—logical structures that can be realized in the form of electronic circuits and that must functionally generate speech objects. We think that a description can be considered accurate (although not natural) if we can create from it a working model capable of fulfilling any part of the functions of verbal communication.

If the problem of linguistics is defined to be the description of language as a structure producing speech, then the aim of MT is to embody this description in algorithms that are realizable on existing electronic computers. By the same token, MT provides linguistics with the experimental basis so necessary to it; in the course of MT, the description of linguistic facts is verified and made more precise, while the methodology of linguistic description itself is perfected. This is the value of MT to linguistics. MT specialists, in turn, should use the language descriptions created by linguistics. Thus, linguistics and MT cannot develop successfully without one another, or without a constant exchange of results and accumulated experience.

While this statement of the interdependence of MT and linguistics is fine in theory, the actual situation is different. A paradox has arisen. On the one hand, MT work has received significant comment in linguistic circles. Special articles on MT are published in such linguistic journals as *Voprosy yazykoznaniya, Word, Modern Language Forum,* and *Babel.* Problems in MT are discussed at international linguistic congresses (the Eighth Congress of Linguists in Oslo, the Fourth Congress of Slavicists in Moscow); moreover, linguists take a considerable part in conferences on MT and related problems (the First Conference on MT, 1952, U.S.A.; the First All-Union Conference on MT, 1958, Moscow; the First Conference on Mathematical Linguistics, 1959, Leningrad, etc.). MT centers have been established at various linguistic institutes and also in universities in several countries, such as the U.S.S.R., the Chinese People's Republic, Czechoslovakia, the U.S.A., and England.

On the other hand, MT remains a highly specialized area that would seem, from its special problems and methods, to be quite separate from theoretical linguistics. At present in MT there is made almost no use of the achievements of contemporary linguistics; whereas pure linguists, while recognizing MT *de jure,* in developing their theories completely ignore MT *de facto.*

Yet MT is not just another special area of linguistics as are studies of Indo-European, Caucasian, and Semitic languages. A specialist in Paleoasiatic languages could easily know nothing about specialized research on Spanish, nor does a linguist studying lexicography need to deal with the problem of case in Caucasian languages. But MT touches equally on *all* specialized areas. The study of various languages and problems, using the approach and methods of MT that have been proven by experiment, will permit a future unification of the science of language. MT is simultaneously both a workshop, where the *methods* of precise linguistic research are perfected independently of the concrete sphere of application of these methods, and an experimental field, where the results are verified by experience. Therefore, it is very important for all linguists to learn as much as they can about MT.

In the following exposition, our purpose is not to describe precisely the bonds between specific questions of MT and the corresponding linguistic problematics; for that we need special research not yet undertaken. Our problem is purely *indicative:* to give a short description of some of the problems of MT that seemed to us to be of interest to linguists.

We have deliberately avoided aspects that, though particularly important for MT, are still too specific and technical at our present level of development. For example, the problem of MT dictionaries and of dictionary search, the problem of a morphological analysis of words during MT, etc., lie here.

## 2. *Two Approaches to Machine Translation*

The problems and methods of MT are variously understood by different researchers. Corresponding to differences in opinion in the MT field, there are two methods of approach, which in foreign literature are sometimes tentatively called the "95 per cent approach" and the "100 per cent approach."

In the first approach, the basic and final purpose of research is the realization of machine translation of scientific-technical texts with the least expenditure of time and effort. The quality of the translation may not be high; it suffices if the greater part of the translated text (hence, the name "95 per cent approach") is understandable to a specialist. For this reason the necessity of complete syntactic analysis is denied; a text is comprehensible to a specialist even with word-for-word translation (at least for certain pairs of languages). The structure of the language does not interest the researchers; the rules for translation are based on instances encountered in the texts analyzed and are gradually broadened by introduction of new texts and discovery of new cases. Such rules may not reflect actual linguistic regularities and may even contradict them. V. H. Yngve has called such rules *"ad hoc* rules."

In the second approach, the study of the general structural regularities of language that form the basis of concrete cases of translation are put foremost. In other words, the researcher tries to explain the possibilities and means used by language to express a particular thought. The rules for translation are formulated with regard to the possibilities explained. Realization of a translation on the machine is considered a means of facilitating knowledge of the structure of language (in the sense indicated above—as a group of laws according to which spoken sequences are constructed). This is necessary, since MT is not considered to be an end in itself but rather the first step in solving a more general problem: how to "teach" electronic computers a whole series of operations using speech, including editing and referencing and the introduction of bibliographic and other corrections to texts.

Much attention has been turned to syntactic and, more recently, to semantic analysis. It is proposed that the possibility of explaining the syntactic (and meaning) structure of a text will allow us not only to improve the quality of machine translations basically but also to automate the operations mentioned earlier that are connected with language.

An important place is assigned to purely linguistic studies of language. Thus, for example, the MT group at the Massachusetts Institute of Technology (U.S.A.) is working out a special structural grammar of German and a parallel, analogous grammar of English in order to determine the correspondence between these languages. "We are looking at language in a new light—through the prism of the 'memory' of a computer," write two members of this group, W. N. Locke and V. H. Yngve, "and we hope that our work on language structure will yield us new and interesting results" [40].

The "100 per cent approach" demands that, although he base his work on some limited text, the linguist use his knowledge of a language fully in formulating rules for translation, turning if necessary to special studies (i.e., introducing additional texts), and that he try to answer all questions cardinally, so that his solution may correspond to the *structural possibilities* of the language. Rules obtained in this way can be called "general rules" (as opposed to the *"ad hoc* rules" mentioned earlier).

The difference between *"ad hoc* rules" and "general rules" can be illustrated by an example from an article by A. Koutsoudas and A. Humecky, "Ambiguity of Syntactic Function Resolved by Linear Context" [38]. In this article, rules are given for determining the syntactic function of Russian short-form adjectives in *-o* (*legko, bystro*) and of comparative adjectives in *-e, -ee* (*legche, bystree*). The rules are based on a large number of examples (approx. 700). They originate from analysis of "linear context" of three words (the short-form, one preceding word, and one following) and ensure correct analysis of nearly all initial examples.

However, D. S. Worth, in his critique of this article [62], cites examples contradicting nearly all of these formulated rules. This is explained, as Worth says, by the fact that Koutsoudas and Humecky had not studied the structural laws of Russian syntax but had simply lumped together the results of a series of translations from Russian to English. In this they used superficial facts—the character of two adjacent words. Study of a larger context would lead to magnification of the number of rules until they enumerated the many individual instances.

Worth's criticisms are valid. The fault does not lie in the fact that Koutsoudas and Humecky did not study some examples, or that they did not have enough examples. If they had tried to find a primary general solution, using only their own material, they would probably have obtained simpler and, moreover, more effective rules. Obviously, "general rules" must be based not on three-word or even larger "linear" context but on knowledge obtained about the whole sentence at the first analysis. (This knowledge is needed to answer many questions in translation and not just to find the syntactic function of the short-form adjective.) Thus, if there is an "obvious" predicate in a sentence (i.e., whether it be a verb in the personal form, or a short-form participle, or a short-form adjective, not neuter and not compared, or a so-called "predicative word" like *nyet* [there is no], *mozhno* [can], etc.), then the form in *-o* (or *-e, -ee*) under consideration can only be a modifier and must be translated as an adverb.[1] We note that it makes no difference in such an approach—as opposed to that taken by Koutsoudas and Humecky—where this "obvious" predicate is found, so no aux-

---

[1] For simplicity of illustration we have omitted the special case of the forms *budet* [will, will be], *bylo* [was] (*budet legko* [(it) will be easy], *bylo vozmozhno* [(it) was possible], etc.).

iliary rules are needed for handling all possible instances of inversion, substitution, etc. Furthermore, if there is no "obvious" predicate in the sentence and the *-o* form under consideration is an adjective of a definite semantic type (e.g., *legko* [ (it) is easy], *estestvenno* [ (it) is natural], *nepravil'no* [ (it) is incorrect] ), and there is an infinitive present in the sentence but no possible infinitive-governing word, then the *-o* form is the predicate (translated into English by "it is" + adj.), and the infinitive is to be connected to the *-o* form (e.g., *legko videt' chto* . . . [it is easy to see that . . . ]). Here again, the mutual word-order has no significance. Other rules for finding the syntactic function of short-form adjectives in *-o* are formed analogously.

Such "general rules" are based on a consideration of the principal possibilities (the semantic types of the short-form adjectives and the presence or absence of certain types of words in the sentence). These rules may be larger in volume than those of Koutsoudas and Humecky, but with a little increase in volume, they increase considerably in their effectiveness. In short, "general rules" can in every case ensure a selection that will be comprehensible (to a human being).

"General rules" are, of course, more interesting to a linguist. In the nature of things, their composition will lead to an exact description of the structure of language, i.e., to the discovery of laws such as those by which this or that content is expressed in language.

In general, the "100 per cent approach," with its broad view of MT, is more closely related to theoretical linguistics and is apparently able to function better in solving the latter's basic problems.

## 3. Syntactic Analysis in Machine Translation

In the first stages of MT's development, the researcher's attention was naturally drawn to the problems of word-for-word translation.

In word-for-word translation, the machine ascribes to each word or form of a word all possible translational equivalents, using a dictionary (or a dictionary and morphological tables).

Linguistic difficulties arising during such a translation are not great and are almost entirely reducible to technical problems. Therefore, it is entirely understandable that the history of practical work in MT began precisely with word-for-word translation.

During the past five or six years, in the U.S.S.R., in the U.S.A., and in England, several experiments in word-for-word translation have been conducted using machines; e.g.: Russian–English translation in the Computation Laboratory of Harvard University (Oettinger's group); French–English in Birkbeck College [23]; French–Russian at the Mathematics Institute of the Academy of Sciences, U.S.S.R. ([6], [7], [8]). (The French–Russian translations were not purely word-for-word; the algorithm employed contextual analysis to distinguish homonyms, etc., though not systematically.) The results have shown that word-for-word translation is suitable as a first approximation for definite pairs of languages and for specialized texts. In some cases, it is useful for direct application.[2] But even in these cases, word-for-word translation is in need of considerable improvement.

On the other hand, for certain pairs of languages (e.g., German–English and English–Russian), word-for-word translation is generally impossible; in such cases, it is necessary to base the translation on a syntactic analysis consisting of a determination of the bonds between words and between parts of the sentence.

*Syntactic analysis gives machine translation an enormous potential for improvement.*

The truth of this fact has long been recognized; one of the first publications on MT (in 1951!) was Oswald and Fletcher's remarkable article on the syntactic analysis of German text for translation into English [47]. The authors had formulated simple and, at the same time, quite effective rules for automatic analysis of the syntactic structure of German sentences. Their approach essentially foreshadowed the direction of research in this area.

In developing the ideas of Oswald and Fletcher, Victor Yngve proposed (in 1955) an interesting methodology that yields a very general solution to the problem of syntactic analysis (see

---

[2] See examples of French–Russian machine translation in [7].

[63] ). Immediately after Yngve, there followed work on various aspects of syntactic analysis by many scientists abroad (the Cambridge MT group in England, the MT group of The RAND Corporation, the collaborators of the Georgetown group in the U.S.A., and others), and in the U.S.S.R. (the MT groups at the Mathematics Institute (MI), the Institute of Precise Mechanics and Computer Techniques (IPMCT), the Linguistics Institute (LI), Leningrad University (LU), and the Academies of Science of Georgia and Armenia).

We shall not give a detailed description of the activities of each group mentioned but shall limit ourselves to a survey of the general state of recent work on the automation of syntactic analysis, citing only the most interesting aspects.

We note especially that in MT the term "syntactic analysis" is rather widely understood and accepted, though insufficiently defined. Syntactic analysis includes the determination of bonds among words, the determination of the character of these bonds, the hierarchy of individual groups of words, the relations among the parts of a complex sentence, etc. Unfortunately, special research that would define the term exactly and establish the boundaries of syntactic analysis has not been undertaken by anyone. We shall, therefore, use the words "syntactic analysis" in the usual broad and rather fuzzy meaning (as primarily intending to determine the bonds among words of a complex sentence).

Many researchers base syntactic analysis on a *list of typical phrase-types* (or constructions). These typical phrases are described in terms of previously defined classes of words. To begin with, word-class attributes are ascribed to all the words in a text with the aid of a special dictionary. Then the machine, comparing the text with the list of phrase-types (i.e., with the list of minimal word-class sequences), finds specific phrases in the text, and thus determines the bonds among the words.

This method was proposed by Victor Yngve (U.S.A.) and, independently, by R. Richens (England). In the U.S.S.R., T. N. Moloshnaya was the first to apply it [17] for constructing an algorithm for English–Russian translation, using a dictionary of "configurations" (as typical phrase-types are called).

A dictionary (list) of elementary syntactic constructions

(about 7,000 entries) is applied in Harper and Hays' Russian—English algorithm [35]. Dictionaries of configurations are applied by the majority of Soviet researchers (the MT groups at LU, IPMCT, LI, and the Georgian Academy of Sciences).

Several basic questions about syntactic analysis, as realized by cutting text into the simplest typical phrases, are considered in T. N. Moloshnaya's work [15] (for English) and in M. V. Sofronov's [20] (for Chinese).

The application of dictionaries of configurations permits the creation of a universal algorithm for syntactic analysis suitable for most, if not all, languages. Between languages, only the content of the configuration dictionary changes, while its general form and the rules for a search of configurations in text, using this dictionary, remain the same. (Analogously, rules for dictionary lookup do not change for various languages.) The general form of a configuration dictionary and a corresponding universal algorithm for syntactic analysis are being developed at LI.

In order to denote typical phrases, it is first necessary to classify words in a way that does not correspond with the traditional division into parts of speech. The number of such classes, in some algorithms, amounts to several dozen or even, in a few cases, to hundreds. Then, the number of typical phrases becomes several thousand.

But an approach is possible in which a single, constant distribution of words into classes in general does not obtain. In place of one class indicator, a series of indicators is written for each word, characterizing all words for all their interesting aspects. Word groupings can be constructed using any combination of indicators. When we need to define a class of words in order to apply some rule, we indicate that class by the necessary attributes and their meanings. Similar indications are included in the formulation of the rules (in the list of configurations); thus, word classes are formed specifically for each rule. This approach is used by LI in its algorithm for syntactic analysis.

This plan for grouping words can be called a "sliding classification." A "sliding classification" is suitable wherever one could, in choosing various combinations of indicators, obtain a large number of word classes of any volume. One can select the indicators so that a class will consist of just one concrete word form; one can also, by taking another combination of indicators, construct a class that includes a very large number of forms. The same words can belong to one class with respect to one set of indicators and to another class with respect to another set.

The "sliding classification" permits a considerable decrease in the number of configurations, to several hundred instead of several thousand. "Sliding classification" is also of considerable interest from a theoretical standpoint. It is possible that the notorious problem of the parts of speech can be studied anew in the light of a consistent development of "sliding classification."

In syntactic analysis, many machine operations, and consequently much time, are spent searching the configuration dictionary. Configurations are compared with the text sequentially, one after the other, until one of them "fits" the phrase being analyzed. Such iteration of configurations seems uneconomical, and we would like to do away with it. An alternate method has been suggested by the collaborators of the Cambridge MT group [44].

Source-text elements that possess the characteristic of predicting groups of a certain type ("structures," as the Cambridge unit has decided to call such groups) are studied. These elements are called "operators." An "operator" has ascribed to it, in the dictionary itself, the number of the structure that it predicts and an indication of its position in this structure. Once the machine encounters this "operator" in text, it immediately turns to the proper structure (in a list of structures) and then searches the text for the remaining elements. Here, the machine does not have to search the whole list of structures.

Similar ideas are being developed by Garvin's group (U.S.A.) [28]. Here, special attention is devoted to so-called "decision points," or "fulcra."

A fulcrum is the element of a syntactic unit that determines the presence and character of this unit. The fulcrum of a sentence is a predicate group, while the fulcrum of the predicate is a verb in the personal form, or a short-form adjective (in Russian), etc. To each fulcrum correspond specific syntactic rules, which are only applied when that fulcrum is discovered. Fulcra are comparable to the operators of the Cambridge group.

In its algorithm for syntactic analysis (of Russian), LI applies a similar method. To each word are ascribed the "addresses" of the first (in list order) configurations into which this word can enter. There are two such "addresses." (Addresses are numbers, the ordinal numbers of the configurations.)

The first "address" is ascribed to the word's root in the dictionary; it is based on the nature of the root itself (its lexical meaning, its capacity to predict some word or form, etc.). The second "address" is produced during morphological analysis; it is based on the form of the word. Reference to the configuration list is always made through the "addresses" of words. Proceeding from left to right through the phrase being analyzed, each word is looked at in turn, and according to its first address, a particular configuration is selected for comparison with the phrase under analysis. For each configuration, "addresses" are indicated for the series of configurations to which the "operating" word must refer, depending on the results of comparison (whether the given configuration had "fit" the phrase being analyzed). After the comparison, the operating word is "re-addressed," then the next word is taken, and the whole process is repeated from the beginning. In this way, search through the whole list of configurations is avoided.[3]

The consequences of syntactic analysis of complex sentences are of special interest. Analysis can proceed by splitting up the component parts of a complex sentence—simple sentences, independent elements, etc. For this purpose, punctuation and certain words, mainly subordinating, are noted specially. Syntactic analysis proper (determination of bonds among words) is conducted within each separate part. Oswald and Fletcher [47] proposed this method; the IPMCT algorithm [18] uses it in analyzing Russian.

Yet another approach is possible: The splitting of a sentence into parts is not effected initially but during determination of the connections among words; this splitting is not the beginning but the end of analysis. This approach is used in the LI algorithm. The phrase being analyzed is split into "segments" according to its punctuation and certain conjunctions (without

---

[3] Many details have been omitted for the sake of simplicity of presentation.

any special analysis of the punctuation or conjunctions themselves), so that the segments do not correspond initially to the
meaningful parts of the phrase but are purely formally separated sections.[4]

Syntactic analysis is performed within each section so obtained with the aid of the configuration list. The initial splitting into segments is necessary to avoid forming false relations
between words in one part of a phrase and words in another
part. However, this splitting, while saving us from false correlations, hinders the determination of many true bonds, since
connected words can belong to different segments at first.

Therefore, when a word is isolated, i.e., when there is no
obligatory bond to be found for it within a segment, then the
segment as a whole takes on a special designation: an indication of what bond has not been made for which word. Thus,
for example, if a transitive verb (e.g., *peremeshchaet* [shifts])
is "separated" from its modifiers (e.g., *elementy* [elements])
as follows:

Segment I
*"Vse elementy*
[All elements],

Segment II
*kotorye prinadlezhat A*
[which belong to A],

Segment III
*eto dvizhenie peremeshchaet v novoe polozhenie . . ."*
[this movement shifts to a new position],

then segment III will be marked with an indication that for its
third word there is "missing" a substantive in the accusative,
and segment I will be marked for the "absence" of a governing
word; i.e., there is an "excess" in segment I of a substantive in
the nominative-accusative case.

---

[4] Several weaknesses (the periods in abbreviations, etc.) were omitted to
simplify the explanation.

The idea of using such designations was advanced by G. B. Chikoidze (in Tbilisi). It has proved fruitful. In its algorithm for analyzing Russian, LI uses only some twenty such designations, indicating the "absence" or the "excess" of words of a particular type in a segment.

When analysis within a segment is finished, segments are compared with each other for resultant designations, so that the "excess" words in certain segments can be connected with the corresponding "unsatisfied" words in other segments. As a result, some of the boundaries between segments are removed and a primary unification of segments obtains. Analysis is repeated, if necessary, with respect to the configurations within the enlarged segments and then a comparison is made of the segments for their designations, etc., until bonds have been established among all the words. Then, the segments will correspond to actual parts of the complex sentence. At this point, on the basis of a consideration of conjunctions and of knowledge of the structure of each segment obtained during analysis, the bonds among the segments and their hierarchy can be established. Here, analysis is completed.

The general organization of the analysis is a separate question.[5] In several projects, separate steps have been used following glossary lookup, consisting of morphological analysis, the finding of idioms, resolution of homographs, treatment of words with various peculiarities, etc. For example, the French–Russian ( [6], [8] ) and Hungarian–Russian [12] algorithms of MI and LI, and the Georgetown University algorithm, "SERNA" ("*S Russkogo Na Anglijskij*"—from Russian to English) [59], are so constructed. During later research it developed, however, that the indicated stages are not basically different from syntactic analysis. Actually, idiom determination in text is the same as the determination of phrase types, and resolution of homonyms is made on the basis of determination of the bonds among words. For this reason, the LI algorithm for syntactic analysis of Russian text includes not only idiom determination but also homonym resolution and treatment of special words. Idioms and the rules for resolving homonyms are

---

[5] About MT analysis, see p. 61 below.

simply special configurations in the general configuration list. This unique approach has allowed a reduction of all procedures to a small group of rote operations, which seemed convenient from the standpoint of constructing an algorithm and of programming.

## 4. The Problem of Meaning in Machine Translation

Since the purpose of machine translation, or translation of any kind, is transformation of text in such a way that its meaning is preserved (more or less), work on MT cannot omit a study of meaning and the level of content of languages. It is sometimes said that MT banishes meaning as an object of research, that the machine cannot make use of meaning characteristics. These assertions are simply untrue. The machine can use any characteristics, including those involving meaning, if only they are clearly described and enumerated beforehand. Isolation and description of the necessary meaning characteristics is, in fact, one of the most important problems in MT. However, the machine cannot at present actually make use of the various *extralinguistic* factors connected with meaning (the correlation of language elements with the objects of real activity, psychological associations, etc.), since such questions have not been treated. The machine operates only with what is immediately contained in the text. Therefore, a purely linguistic description of meanings must be made for MT: The meaning of an element is describable by its substitutability (how it fits into synonymous series or into groups of translational equivalents in various languages)[6] and by its distribution (the appearance of the element in specified kinds of context). This approach is not the special property of MT; in fact, meaning must be studied by the same methods in linguistics as well. Here, of course, the productivity of other approaches is not denied, particularly the psychological approach. It is important only to distinguish clearly the linguistic and nonlinguistic approaches. MT forces this distinction to be made very logically.

---

[6] See below, pp. 65-66, on the "thesaurus method."

In the light of MT studies, we can consider anew such classic linguistic questions as that of homonymy and synonymy. Thus, from the MT point of view, one can speak of homonymy when the same sequence of elements (e.g., letters) must, for the sake of satisfactory translation, be treated variously. The distinction between homonymy and polysemy is not made at this time, since it makes no difference to the machine at MT's present stage of development whether or not there is any connection in meaning between two possible translations of a particular word. Later, when we have more complete systems of "semantic factors" (see p. 66), this distinction will become essential, and its value will be exactly measured by a group of general "semantic factors" constituting the meanings of the two words compared.

Unfortunately, general theoretical questions connected with research on the meaning aspect of language for MT purposes have not been treated at all. For this reason, we shall limit our discussion to one of the practical aspects of the broad theme: "meaning in MT." We have in mind the problem of multivalence.

Elimination of the multivalence of language elements (words, grammatical indicators), in its broadest sense (including the various cases of homonymy, see above), is a basic problem of MT in its more general form. Multivalence on the MT level means the presence of several translations; the removal of multivalence is the choice of the necessary equivalent from among the several possible ones. If multivalence did not exist, and the machine did not have to make such a choice, then MT would be reduced to very simple transformations.

The problem of multivalence of language elements (mainly that of words) is constantly being discussed in MT studies. Many suggestions have been made concerning automatic elimination of lexical multivalence. They can be grouped as follows:

(1) Limitation of multivalence according to subject-matter. It is proposed to apply special idioglossaries in which words are given only the meanings applicable to them within a given field. One could also furnish each translation of a word with a code indicating the area in which it is applicable.

(2) Reducing the number of translations by choosing the most general translations (i.e., those that can be stretched to fit all instances and still not confuse the meaning of a text, though weakening the style) or the most probable (the most frequent) translations.

(3) Context analysis. Interesting research by A. Kaplan [37] has shown experimentally that context, even when understood to be simply *adjacent words,* possesses considerable "force" for removing multivalence. Obviously, if by the context of a multivalent word we mean "words immediately connected syntactically with the given word," then the "differentiating force" of such context will be still greater. For just this reason, V. H. Yngve proposed a solution of the problem of lexical multivalence based on a previously developed syntactic structure for the sentence being translated [64]. This solution seems to be the most productive. First, the attributes of various meaning-categories (object, person, action, condition, organization, etc.) are ascribed to words; the translation of the multivalent word is chosen using rules indicating which of these attributes in words syntactically connected with the given word correspond to the choice of this translation. Something similar is done in applying the "thesaurus method" (see pp. 65-66).

A special case of the use of context for removing multivalence is the discovery of idioms having a special translation.

(4) The most "powerful," but at the same time an extremely complex, means of removing ambiguity consists of giving the machine so many designations of meaning and the connections among them that it can "understand" the content of a text (in the broad sense of the word). Then, besides syntactic bonds, the machine can in translating make use of the meaning relations—rules showing the permissible combinations of semantic designations. Given such a capability, the machine can correct faulty text (with typographical errors, omissions, faults) by the meaning.

Special work is being done for transition to such semantic analysis with the purpose of obtaining a sufficiently full collection of the simplest semantic elements, such that through combinations of these, one can represent the meanings of any language units. Such elements have been called "semantic factors" [3]. Semantic factors are necessary not only for MT but also for many other operations on text, especially referencing and correction, as well as for encoding scientific-technical information to be stored and operated upon by so-called information machines.

Several groups are working on extracting semantic factors for texts in various fields of knowledge. We cite in particular J. Perry and A. Kent's group in the U.S.A., the Cambridge group in England, and the MT Laboratory at the First Moscow State Pedagogical Institute of Foreign Languages.

We shall not treat in detail the question of a method for expanding meanings into semantic factors. Basically, this method consists of defining semantic factors by determining the correspondences among the various elements both within one language and between languages. Later, when we discuss interlingua and, in particular, the specification of the semantic elements of an interlingua, we shall describe one of the methods applied—the so-called "thesaurus method" (see pp. 65-66).

The construction of sets of semantic factors is especially valuable for linguistics because it permits the study of meanings as systems, i.e., as units formed by definite rules from a small number of simpler elements.

## 5. Interlingua

The problem of interlingua for MT, formulated at an earlier stage of MT's development, is frequently discussed in the literature and in MT publications.[7] Nevertheless, it is far from a final solution; moreover, complete clarity has not as yet been attained in several general representations of interlingua. We shall confine ourselves to a short résumé of some of the ideas expressed on this subject.

In nonliteral MT (and frequently also in word-for-word MT —see V. H. Yngve's remarks on p. 64), the translation process is separated into two stages: analysis and synthesis.

In *analysis,* specific data about the text being translated (information about the translations of words, their morphological forms, the connections among words, etc.) are extracted from

---

[7] E. Reifler's paper at the first MT conference, 1952 [51].

it. These data express the same meaning[8] as the input text but explicitly and unambiguously, unlike the language elements, which are connected with the meaning inexplicitly and ambiguously (meaning may, for example, be expressed by the relative distribution of the language elements). The set of data we can obtain from analysis is so arranged that, by referring to it, we can construct an output text. Constructing texts from analysis data is the converse of analysis and is called *synthesis*.

For every language, data are collected consisting of the characteristics needed for a unique and explicit expression of the meaning of texts in this language. These characteristics are, on the one hand, the goal and result of analysis and, on the other, the raw material for synthesis. The set of characteristics is developed for a concrete language with the introduction of its grammatical categories and others necessary and convenient for translation of the information. This set is, in fact, the unique "intermediary language."

In binary translation (from one language to another in a given direction), analysis of the input language is performed immediately in terms of the characteristics of the output; this is so-called "dependent analysis." For example, in French–Russian translation, the cases of nouns are immediately determined during analysis of the French text, since these characteristics are needed for synthesizing the Russian text.

But in multiple translation (from many languages to many others in any direction), such an approach is not very useful; as many analysis algorithms are needed for each input language as there are output languages proposed (each algorithm leads from the text in the input language to the characteristics of one of the output languages). Thus, in "dependent analysis" ten languages would need ninety analysis algorithms (nine "dependent analyses" for every language) and ten synthesis algorithms (since synthesis is always independent).

In order to avoid a large number of algorithms, we can apply "independent analysis": For each language there is just one analysis algorithm leading from the text in the input language to the characteristics of this language, and one synthesis algorithm performing the converse operation. In addition, there is

---

[8] Or rather, almost the same; some loss of information may occur.

a set of rules by which the characteristics of the input language derived from analysis are transformed into the characteristics of the output language needed for synthesis. This set of rules is also an interlingua. For example, the interlingua of the MT group at M.I.T. ([63], [64]) can be understood in this way.

There exists yet another approach, as follows: After the necessary correspondences have been made between the sets of characteristics of concrete languages, these sets are united in a particular manner into one maximal set (macroset) that suffices for the unique expression of the meaning of a text in any of the input languages. This universal set of characteristics is regarded as an interlingua. Then, analysis will always lead directly from the input text to universal characteristics, and synthesis begins immediately with these characteristics. In this approach, a special stage of transformation (between analysis and synthesis) is apparently practically nonexistent, because of the inclusion of aspects of transformation in analysis and synthesis.

The interlingua, in this sense, is nothing other than a notational system applicable for a unique, explicit, and sufficiently suitable expression of the meaning contained in texts in languages subjected to translation.

This position is entirely in agreement with the principles of the "100 per cent approach" to MT mentioned above, which requires that translation be realized "by the meaning," i.e., that the meaning be extracted from the text being translated, written in a special, standard form, and then that the output-language text be constructed only according to this meaning, independent of the input text.

Before proceeding to the question of the form of an interlingua, we shall touch, in passing, on the necessity for an interlingua that has arisen in the literature.

The opponents of interlingua have indicated that its advantages (reducing the number of analysis algorithms) can only become effective for a rather large number of languages, while for three or four—and especially for only two—languages, the interlingua is not at all necessary, since it yields little advantage in the number of algorithms and complicates each of them. However, as we have said earlier, in binary translation, too, a certain "intermediary language" is applied—e.g., the characteristics of the output text obtained from analysis. V. H. Yngve has shown that nearly all algorithms apply an "intermediary language" even if inexplicitly and unconsciously. For example, in the French–English algorithm of Birkbeck College (in England), the dictionary is divided into French and English parts. Each French word has stored with it not its English equivalent but only the address of the location of its equivalent. The set of addresses in fact represents the "intermediary" or transitional language, as Yngve has called it. Such a "language" permits the writing of language information in the machine in the most economical form and is convenient in machine operations. Since these "intermediary languages" exist, they must be applied deliberately. It now becomes apparent that interlingua is necessary both in binary translation and in multiple, and Yngve's group (at M.I.T.) is occupied with developing an interlingua for German–English translation.

Of course, there remains the purely terminological question: Should one call just any "intermediary" (transition) language an interlingua?

Still another argument is used against interlingua: Interlingua, while decreasing the general number of analysis algorithms from $n + n \, (n - 1)$ to $2n$, i.e., in the ratio $n^2 : 2n = n/2$ (for twenty languages, a tenfold reduction), seems to lead to greater complexity of the algorithms. But this assertion is rather indefinite, for there does not exist at present a way of evaluating the "complexity" or the "simplicity" of algorithms. Moreover, no one has yet compared algorithms constructed in conjunction with an interlingua with algorithms in which interlingua is not used at all (if the latter, in fact, exists; see above).

At present, the need for interlingua as such is recognized by all groups in the U.S.S.R., by the researchers in the Cambridge group in England, by V. H. Yngve's group in the U.S.A., and by others. However, the form of the interlingua is not as yet decided upon.

In the literature four types of interlinguas are discussed:

(1) One of the natural languages may be used as an interlingua (e.g., the language of the country in which particular MT algorithms are being created). But since the interlingua must ensure a monovalent, explicit, and maximally economical

notation for meaning extracted from the input text, and no natural language satisfies these requirements, this method apparently is not being followed consistently by anyone in practice.

(2) The interlingua may consist of a standardized and simplified natural language. An example of this is the "Model English" proposed by Stuart C. Dodd [41].

(3) The interlingua may be one of the artificial international languages, such as Esperanto or Interlingua. The use of Interlingua as an interlingua has been studied by A. Gode [31].

(4) However, a method more likely to be useful is the creation of specially adapted artificial languages for MT. Pioneer groups dealing directly with the problem of interlingua (at Cambridge, at Leningrad University, and at the MT Federation in Moscow) have all come to the same conclusion: construction of an interlingua as a system of correspondences among natural languages (for simplicity in presentation, we shall not touch upon the differences existing among the approaches used by the groups mentioned). This viewpoint is most fully presented in the publications of the Cambridge group in presenting the so-called "thesaurus method" ( [42], [43] ).

A thesaurus is a particular kind of dictionary in which words are grouped into thematic classes that are divided into sections and, further, into categories.[9] In the most famous dictionary of this kind—*Roget's International Thesaurus of English Words and Phrases*—there are six classes, twenty-four sections, and more than 1,000 categories. For example: The class "Space" includes the sections "General," "Measurement," "Form," "Motion"; the section "Motion" is divided into the categories "Change of Position," "Rest," "Land Travel," "Flying (air travel)," "Traveller," "Sailor," "Aeronaut," etc. In addition to being joined into thematic groups, the words are listed alphabetically, and each is assigned numbers (or headings, called "heads") for the thematic groups to which it belongs.

A word can belong simultaneously to several groups, as in the case of homonyms ("rock," as *skala* [cliff, crag], or as *kachat'*

---

[9] The term "thesaurus" is also used to refer to dictionaries in which the lexical system of a language is presented quite thoroughly.

[to rock] ), or in the case of polysemy ("rod," as *sterzhen'* [stirring rod], or as *rozga* [birch rod] ).

The entry for the word "flat" from *Roget's Thesaurus* is:

| | |
|---|---|
| *flat* | 172—inertia |
| | 191—story, level |
| | 207—low |
| | 213—horizontal |
| | 223—color |
| | etc. |

In other words, every word has assigned to it series of synonyms with which it is associated (in various meanings); a series of synonyms (or rather, the group nearest to the word in meaning) forms a thematic category.

Thesauri can also be interlingual. In that case, groups of words from several languages, similar in meaning, are joined into the same thematic category.

Translation of lexical content is done in two stages when an interlingual thesaurus is used:

(1) There may be several thematic-category numbers with the word to be translated, and the necessary number (that most suitable in the given context) is chosen first; for this purpose, sets of such numbers are compared for syntactically connected words, and common numbers are selected.

(2) All words in the output language that are near in meaning, and might *in a particular context* be the equivalents of a given word, are pulled according to their thematic-category number. The choice of the proper equivalent from among several possible ones is made according to special rules belonging entirely to the output language.

In the specially constructed thesaurus, where groups of words in various languages are, taken as a whole, mutually and uniquely related to one another, thematic-category numbers may be thought of as *the words of an interlingua.*

The relations among semantic elements (words) in the interlingua can be expressed by the same indexes, with symbols for the related elements [55], or with parentheses grouping pairs of elements—the defining and the defined—so that a pair included in parentheses may be thought of as a single element

[49]. The interlingua of the Cambridge group does not have grammar in the general sense (number, case, tense).

We shall not describe in detail the approaches of the Leningrad and Moscow groups to the problem of interlingua but shall refer the reader to the relevant publications: [1], [2], [3], [13]. We shall only note that workers in the Leningrad group have already obtained practical results. They have developed an experimental version of interlingua for a series of natural languages (Russian, Czech, English, Indonesian, and others), and soon an experimental machine translation should be realized from any one of these languages to another, using interlingua. Along with the interlingua created by determination of the correspondences among natural languages, another type of interlingua is possible: purely logical, developed from analysis of the content of some science but without introduction of data from natural languages. Apparently, the members of Perry and Kent's group in the U.S.A. and of the Electromodeling Laboratory of VINITI[10] in the U.S.S.R. are following this method.

## 6. Formalization of Algorithm Notation

In conjunction with the problem of interlingua, much attention has been drawn to the question of a specialized "language" for MT algorithm notation. Because such a "language" permits a generally known standardization of algorithms, it simplifies their construction and control and, most of all, essentially simplifies their programming by permitting a transition to automatic programming. Formal notation for algorithms presupposes the use of a small number of precisely defined expressions (commands, questions, etc.). A standard program is made for the realization of each such expression. Then, since all expressions have a standard form, the machine can decipher these expressions and replace them with the corresponding programs. In other words, automatic programming is nothing other than a machine translation of the MT algorithm itself from the

---

[10] [VINITI = All-Union Institute of Scientific and Technical Information.—Tr.]

language in which it was written by the analyst to the internal language (the so-called "order code") of a particular machine. Naturally, the more standardized and regular the initial notation of the algorithm, the more simply the corresponding translation is realized.

Several MT groups apply a logico-mathematical symbolism as algorithm notation for finding predicates, augmented by a series of conditional designations (the Harvard and Georgetown groups in the U.S.A.). A special symbolic language, which includes designations of language elements and of the operations being performed, has been developed by the Leningrad group. This language has been proved in practice—for writing several algorithms (11).

The language presented by Yngve for writing algorithms (his *programming language*)—COMIT [65]—has still another structure. The essence of Yngve's idea is that a single standard form is used for writing the rules composing the program. Each rule has five parts. The number of the rule is written in part I, and part V contains the number of the rule to which to proceed after carrying out the operations required by the present rule. In part II are indicated the elements (words, parts of words, etc.) or attributes on which to perform the operation; what is to be done with these elements or attributes (substitution, erasure, or addition of elements; ascription or erasure of attributes; etc.) is shown in part III. Part IV defines the boundary of the algorithm to which the particular rule applies, and sometimes contains an indication about a transition to this or that subrule of the rule (this indication to be used by a special part of the algorithm, called the "dispatcher").

COMIT is used by the MT group at M.I.T. for writing algorithms, in particular, a German–English algorithm. COMIT is also beginning to be applied by several other groups in the U.S.A.

The so-called "operator notation" for MT algorithms developed by O. S. Kulagina ( [4], [5] ), in addition to introducing a standard form of rules, contains a whole list of allowable operations—operators. An operator is a small algorithm handling one precisely specified part of a problem: e.g., verifying the presence of an attribute, noting an attribute, searching for words with particular attributes. The operator has a *fixed* internal structure but *variable* parameters; thus, one and the same operator can, for example, verify the presence of various attributes for various words. Kulagina's operators are like standard details [i.e., components] from which the MT algorithm is formulated.

On the basis of the analytic part of the French–Russian algorithm ( [6], [8] ), Kulagina selected seventeen operators: three different verification operators, two different search operators, an erasure operator, an operator for inserting words, etc. These operators are not all bound to the specifics of the French language and can be applied in algorithms for a number of other languages.

Thanks to the application of operators, the logical structure of the algorithms becomes quite explicit, and their construction is thus simplified. Operator notation permits a transition to the automatic programming of algorithms. Kulagina has performed an experiment in automatic programming of part of the Hungarian–Russian algorithm [12]; in five minutes, the machine constructed five programs that would have taken twenty to thirty man-days.

The idea of operator notation seems highly productive; at present, and as a continuation of Kulagina's work, a compilation of so-called algorithm operators is being made [14]. Operators connected with programming technique, with peculiarities of realization, are excluded from this compilation, and new operators resulting from the creation of a more complex type of algorithm are introduced.

## 7. The Interaction of Man and Machine during MT

This question has many interesting facets of which we shall mention several here.

Man can participate in the process of MT either by initially preparing the text to aid the machine in handling multivalence, etc. (pre-editing), or by the necessary polishing of the rough translation made by the machine (postediting). The question of the usefulness of pre- or postediting (or of both) still remains unsolved. Most researchers are inclined to prefer postediting, though there are no exact figures on this. Evidently, Y. Bar-Hillel was right [22] in emphasizing the importance of pre- or postediting and in indicating that, since high-quality, *fully* automatic translation is not at first achievable, it would be desirable to organize an intelligent interaction between man and machine and to arrive as quickly as possible at partially automatic mass translation. This would permit the accumulation of valuable experience for the further development of machine translation.

Electronic computers can be successfully applied to assist humans in varied research on language. During the 1950's, several experiments were conducted in which the machine helped to produce, with minimal expenditure of time and effort, listings ("concordances") of large quantities of text: of the Bible, of the preachings of Thomas Aquinas, of the Dead Sea Scrolls, etc. (see papers by Cook [25], Tasman [57], and Ellison).

All of these experiments demonstrated the usefulness of computers in various kinds of lexicographic work (extracting dictionary materials from text, sorting these materials, etc.), and for all sorts of statistical counts: machine-aided calculation of the frequencies of letters and morphemes, words, and even syntactic constructions; thus, the National Bureau of Standards produced a frequency count for various kinds of syntactic constructions for English using the SEAC [56]. Such application of machines has great value not only for MT but also for linguistics as a whole.

Experiments involving "learning machines" are especially interesting; "learning" is used here in its broadest conditional sense. The simplest such experiment involves a machine's completing its own dictionary independently during the translation. A word in the text to be translated, but not in the dictionary, is pulled from the text along with the defining context and an indication of its text location; then it is placed in the dictionary in alphabetic order. A man then writes the necessary dictionary information (in the MT groups of Harvard University, U.S.A., and at Birkbeck College, England).

In the MT studies being conducted by the group at The RAND Corporation (U.S.A.), the machine is expanding the list of elementary syntactic constructions available to it.[11] Sequences of words not corresponding to any in the list are printed out by the machine along with their text location and are classified by specific characteristics for later study by linguists.

We should note experiments in applying the machine for automation and even for automatically writing MT algorithms. For example, a plan developed at the Computation Laboratory of Harvard University is as follows. A word-for-word Russian— English translation is made with the aid of the machine. This translation is corrected by a posteditor using special instructions prescribing definite actions and the writing of changes introduced in a standard form. The postedited translation is again input to the machine, which compares it with the initial (word-for-word) translation, discovers the differences, collects and classifies them, and then, on the basis of an analysis of these differences, constructs an algorithm capable of introducing into the word-for-word translation the same changes that had been written in by the posteditor. This algorithm is included in the initial stage of the translation, and initial translation improves. Now the posteditor receives something better than a word-for-word translation. Once again he corrects the text, which is again input to the machine, and the cycle is repeated until the quality of translations output by the machine satisfies the posteditor. Thus the machine is able, as it were, to "learn" by analyzing and imitating the actions of the posteditor ([30], [36], [45]).

## 8. Some Facts about Work in MT

In the preceding sections no exhaustive characterization of all the basic problems of MT is to be found. These sections are meant only to give the reader a general idea of the state of machine translation.

Machine translation is a little over ten years old. The idea of mechanizing translation from one language to another was expressed by the Soviet inventor P. P. Troyansky as far back as

---

[11] [In fact, the machine has not done more than aid in the expansion.—Tr.]

1933; in that year Troyansky obtained a patent for his translating machine.[12] But at that time Troyansky's ideas did not receive the necessary development. After the invention of high-speed electronic computers, the idea of mechanizing translation with their aid arose once again (1946, Weaver and Booth); in 1949, the first research was begun (in the U.S.A.). In 1952, the Massachusetts Institute of Technology called the First Conference on MT, and from then on the number of publications dedicated to MT questions has risen steadily. In the beginning of 1954, IBM conducted an experiment in Russian–English translation on the IBM 701. Thus, the possibility of MT was proven in practice. In the U.S.S.R., work on MT began in 1954, and in 1956, English–Russian and French–Russian translations were realized. Since 1955, more new groups have joined in MT research. The scope of the work has been increasing steadily.

At present, machine translation is being pursued in the following countries: the U.S.S.R., the U.S.A., England, Japan, China, Czechoslovakia, Italy, France, Sweden, Israel, Mexico, and India. Only the U.S.A. has more than ten groups participating. These groups are concentrated in the larger research centers, such as the universities—Harvard, Georgetown, Washington, Chicago, M.I.T., and others; and in corporations—RAND and Ramo-Wooldridge; etc. The largest of the groups includes dozens of workers. There are two groups at work in England (Birkbeck College and Cambridge University[13]). In the U.S.S.R., five groups in Moscow are working on MT and related problems (at the Pedagogical Institute of Foreign Languages and at four institutes of the Academy of Sciences: the Mathematics Institute, the Institute of Precise Mechanics and Computer Techniques, the Electromodeling Laboratory of VINITI, and the Institute of Linguistics); and there is one group in each of five other cities: Leningrad (Leningrad University), Kiev (Kiev University and the Computational Cen-

---

[12] See the brochure "Perevodnaya mashina P. P. Troyanskogo" ["The Translation Machine of P. P. Troyansky"], published in 1959 by the Izd-vo Akademii nauk SSSR, Moscow, pp. 1–40 (translated in JPRS 3532, U.S. Joint Publications Research Service, July, 1960, pp. 1–39).

[13] [The Cambridge Language Research Unit is actually independent of the University.—Tr.]

ter of the Academy of Sciences), Erevan (Computational Center of the Armenian S.S.R.), Tbilisi (Institute of Automatics and Telemechanics of the Georgian Academy of Sciences), and Gorky (Radiophysical Institute).

In the U.S.A. and in the U.S.S.R., special journals are published on MT: *Mechanical Translation* (M.I.T.) and *Mashinnyj perevod i prikladnaya lingvistika [Machine Translation and Applied Linguistics]* (Moscow Institute of Foreign Languages).

The group of languages being machine translated has greatly increased. Whereas attention at first was primarily concentrated on Russian and English, work is now being conducted on MT in the following languages as well: French, German, Italian, Chinese, Hindi, Japanese, Indonesian, Arabic, Hungarian, Czech, Georgian, Armenian, and others.

From 1957 to 1960, quite a few experimental machine translations were made both in the U.S.S.R. and abroad. At the Mathematics Institute, French–English translation experiments have been conducted that include translations of selected running texts; examples of phrases translated by the machine appear in [7] and [23]. Recently, English–Russian translation experiments have been begun there, too.

Experimental Russian–English translations have been made by various groups in the U.S.A. The Harvard and Georgetown groups and that at The RAND Corporation conduct these experiments more or less regularly.

MT experiments have been conducted successfully from French to English, from Russian and English to Chinese, from English to Japanese, and from English to Czech in England, China, Japan, and Czechoslovakia.

The experience accumulated as a result of these experiments has permitted the serious undertaking of *mass* MT. Further development of the theory of MT needed here will lead to the presentation of new and interesting problems and will have considerable influence on linguistics as a whole.[14]

---

[14] The author expresses his sincere gratitude to V. V. Ivanov, A. A. Reformatskij, O. S. Kulagina, and L. N. Iordanskaya for their valuable notes and advice.

## BIBLIOGRAPHY FOR CHAPTERS III AND IV

1. Andreyev, N. D., "Mashinnyj perevod i problema yazyka-posrednika" ["Machine Translation and the Problem of an Intermediary Language"], *Voprosy yazykoznaniya*, Vol. 6, 1957, pp. 117–121.

2. ———, "Meta-yazyk mashinnogo perevoda i ego primenenie" ["A Metalanguage of Machine Translation and Its Use"], in *Materialy po mashinnomu perevodu*, Vol. I, Izd-vo Leningradskogo gosudarstvennogo universiteta, Leningrad, 1958, pp. 40–60. (Translated: JPRS 2150, U.S. Joint Publications Research Service, February, 1960, pp. 26–40.)

3. Ivanov, V. V., "Lingvisticheskie voprosy sozdaniya mashinnogo yazyka dlya informatsionnoj mashiny" ["Linguistic Problems in the Creation of a Machine Language for Information Machines"], in *Materialy po mashinnomu perevodu*, Vol. I, Izd-vo Leningradskogo gosudarstvennogo universiteta, Leningrad, 1958, pp. 10–39. (Translated: JPRS 2150, U.S. Joint Publications Research Service, February, 1960, pp. 6–25.)

4. Kulagina, O. S., "Ob operatornom opisanii algoritmov perevoda i avtomatizatsii protsessa ikh programmirovaniya" ["Operator Description of Algorithms for Translation and Automation of the Process of Programming Them"], *Problemy kibernetiki,* Vol. 2, 1959, pp. 289–302.

5. ———, "Operatornoe opisanie algoritmov perevoda" ["Operator Description of Algorithms for Translation"], *Mashinnyj perevod i prikladnaya lingvistika*, No. 2(9), 1959, pp. 6–22, and No. 3 (10), 1959, pp. 3–34. (Translated: JPRS 3599, U.S. Joint Publications Research Service, August, 1960, pp. 5–15.)

6. ———, "O mashinnom perevode s frantsuzskogo yazyka na russkij, I" ["French-to-Russian Machine Translation, I"], *Problemy kibernetiki*, Vol. 3, 1960, pp. 181–208.

7. ———, and G. V. Vakulovskaya, "Opytnye perevody s frantsuzskogo yazyka na russkij na mashine 'Strela' " ["Experimental French–Russian Translations on the Machine 'Strela' "], *Problemy kibernetiki*, Vol. 2, 1959, pp. 283–288.

8. Kulagina, O. S., and I. A. Mel'chuk, "Mashinnyj perevod s frantsuzskogo yazyka na russkij" ["French-to-Russian Machine Translation"], *Voprosy yazykoznaniya*, Vol. 5, No. 5, 1956, pp. 111–121.

9. Liu Yüng, Ts'uan, "Issledovatel'skaya rabota v oblasti MP v

Kitajskoj Narodnoj Respublike" ["Research on Machine Translation in the Chinese People's Republic"], *Voprosy yazykoznaniya*, Vol. 8, No. 5, 1959, pp. 102–104.

10. ———, "Vopros o poryadke slov i ego reshenie pri MP s russkogo yazyka na kitajskij" ["Problems of Word-Order in Russian–Chinese Machine Translation and Their Solutions"], *Yu-yen Yen-chiu*, No. 4, 1959, pp. 107–116. (Translated: JPRS 3356, U.S. Joint Publications Research Service, June, 1960.)

11. "Voprosy statistiki rechi" ["Questions on the Statistics of Speech"], *Materialy po mashinnomu perevodu*, Vol. I, Leningrad State University Press, Leningrad, 1958.

12. Mel'chuk, I. A., "O mashinnom perevode s vengerskogo yazyka na russkij" ["Machine Translation from Hungarian to Russian"], *Problemy kibernetiki*, Vol. 1, 1958, pp. 222–264. (Translated: JPRS 646–D, U.S. Joint Publications Research Service, April 10, 1959.)

13. ———, "Raboty po mashinnomu perevodu v SSSR" ["Work on Machine Translation in the USSR"], *Vestnik AN SSSR*, No. 2, April 24, 1959, pp. 43–47. (Translated: JPRS 662, U.S. Joint Publications Research Service.)

14. ———, "O standartnykh operatorakh dlya algoritma avtomaticheskogo analiza russkogo nauchnogo teksta" ["Standard Operators for Automatic Analysis of Russian Scientific Text"], not yet published.

15. Moloshnaya, T. N., "Nekotorye voprosy sintaksisa v svyazi s mashinnym perevodom s anglijskogo yazyka na russkij" ["Certain Questions of Syntax in Connection with Machine Translation from English into Russian"], *Voprosy yazykoznaniya*, Vol. 6, No. 4, 1957, pp. 92–97.

16. ———, "Voprosy razlicheniya omonimov pri mashinnom perevode s anglijskogo yazyka na russkij" ["Problems in Distinguishing Homonyms in Machine Translation from English into Russian"], *Problemy kibernetiki*, Vol. 1, 1958, pp. 216–221. (Translated: JPRS 646–D, U.S. Joint Publications Research Service, April, 1959.)

17. ———, "Algoritm perevoda s anglijskogo yazyka na russkij" ["An Algorithm for Translating the English Language into Russian"], *Problemy kibernetiki*, Vol. 3, 1960, pp. 209–272. (Translated: JPRS 6492, U.S. Joint Publications Research Service, December 29, 1960, pp. 41–123.)

18. Nikolayeva, T. M., *Analiz russkogo predlozheniya [An Analysis of Russian Prepositions]*, Institut tochnoj mekhaniki i

vychislitel'noj tekhniki, Izd-vo Akademii nauk SSSR, Moscow, 1958.

19. Rozentsvejg, V. Yu., "Raboty po mashinnomu perevodu s inostrannykh yazykov na russkij i s russkogo na inostrannye v Sovetskom Soyuze" ["Work in the Soviet Union on Machine Translation from Foreign Languages into Russian and from Russian into Foreign Languages"], *Reports of the Fourth International Conference of Slavicists,* Moscow, 1958. (Translated by Lew Micklesen, University of Washington.)

20. Sofronov, M. V., "Obshchie printsipy mashinnogo perevoda s kitajskogo yazyka" ["General Principles of Machine Translation from the Chinese Language"], *Voprosy yazykoznaniya,* Vol. 7, No. 2, 1958, pp. 116–121. (Translated: JPRS DC–319, U.S. Joint Publications Research Service, November 14, 1958.)

21. Bar-Hillel, Y., "The Present State of Research on Mechanical Translation," *American Documentation,* Vol. 2, 1951, pp. 229–237.

22. ———, *Report on the State of Machine Translation in the United States and Great Britain* (mimeographed), Hebrew University, Jerusalem, Israel, February 15, 1959.

23. Booth, A. D., "General Applications of Digital Computers," *Journal of the Institution of Electrical Engineers,* New Series: Vol. 3, No. 36, December, 1957, pp. 629–636.

24. ———, L. Brandwood, and J. Cleave, *Mechanical Resolution of Linguistic Problems,* Butterworth and Co., Ltd., London, 1958.

25. Cook, C. M., "Automation Comes to the Bible [Univac Helps Compile Concordance]," *Computers and Automation,* Vol. 7, March, 1958, pp. 16–18.

26. Delavenay, É., *La Machine à Traduire,* "Que sais-je?" series, No. 834, Presses Universitaires de France, Paris, 1959.

27. Garvin, P., "Linguistic Analysis and Translation Analysis," *Report of the Eighth Annual Round Table Meeting on Linguistics and Language Studies,* Monograph Series on Language and Linguistics, No. 10, Georgetown University Press, Washington, D.C., 1957, pp. 19–38.

28. ———, D. Lochak, M. Mathiot, and C. Montgomery, *Report of Group II—The Georgetown University Project in Machine Translation Research,* Seminar Work Paper MT–73, Georgetown University Press, Washington, D.C., 1957.

29. Giuliano, V. E., "An Experimental Study of Automatic Language Translation," *Mathematical Linguistics and Auto-*

*matic Translation* (Report No. NSF–1), The Computation Laboratory, Harvard University, Cambridge, Massachusetts, January, 1959.

30. ———, "A Formula Finder for the Automatic Synthesis of Translation Algorithms," *Mathematical Linguistics and Automatic Translation* (Report No. NSF–2), The Computation Laboratory, Harvard University, Cambridge, Massachusetts, March, 1959, pp. IX:1–41.

31. Gode, A., "The Signal System in Interlingua—A Factor in Mechanical Translation," *Mechanical Translation*, Vol. 2, No. 3, December, 1955, pp. 55–60.

32. Harper, K. E., "The Mechanical Translation of Russian, A Preliminary Study," *Modern Language Forum*, Vol. 38, No. 3–4, 1953, pp. 12–29.

33. ———, "Semantic Ambiguity," *Mechanical Translation*, Vol. 4, No. 3, December, 1957, pp. 68–69.

34. ———, "Contextual Analysis," *Mechanical Translation*, Vol. 4, No. 3, December, 1957, pp. 70–75.

35. ———, and D. G. Hays, *The Use of Machines in the Construction of a Grammar and Computer Program for Structural Analysis*, The RAND Corporation, P–1588, 1959. [Published in the *Proceedings of the International Conference on Information Processing*, UNESCO, 1960.]

36. Jones, P. E., "A Feedback System for the Harvard Automatic Translator," *Mathematical Linguistics and Automatic Translation* (Report No. NSF–3), The Computation Laboratory, Harvard University, Cambridge, Massachusetts, August, 1959, pp. XIV:1–60.

37. Kaplan, A., "An Experimental Study of Ambiguity and Context," *Mechanical Translation*, Vol. 2, No. 2, November, 1955, pp. 39–46.

38. Koutsoudas, A., and A. Humecky, "Ambiguity of Syntactic Function Resolved by Linear Context," *Word*, Vol. 13, No. 3, December, 1957, pp. 403–414.

39. Lehiste, J., "Order of Subject and Predicate in Scientific Russian," *Mechanical Translation*, Vol. 4, No. 3, December, 1957, pp. 66–67.

40. Locke, W. N., and V. H. Yngve, "Research in Translation by Machine at M.I.T.," *Reports for the Eighth International Congress of Linguists*, Vol. 11, University of Oslo Press, Oslo, Norway, pp. 315–318.

41. Locke, W. N., and A. D. Booth, eds., *Machine Translation of Languages* (14 essays, with historical review), John Wiley

& Sons, Inc., New York, 1955, and M.I.T. Technical Press, 1955; Chapman and Hall, Ltd., London, 1955; Izd-vo inostr. lit., Moscow, 1957.

42. Masterman, M., "The Thesaurus in Syntax and Semantics," *Mechanical Translation,* Vol. 4, No. 1–2, November, 1957, pp. 35–43.

43. ———, "What Is a Thesaurus?," *Essays on and in Machine Translation by Cambridge Language Research Unit,* Cambridge University Press, Cambridge, England, 1959.

44. ———, A. Parker-Rhodes, and M. Hoskyns, "Skeletal Program for the Translation of *'dan c liang ze'* (The Comparative Analysis of 'However, these two, in appearance and solubility, are slightly unlike' [original Chinese]): An Account of the Pilot Project of the Cambridge Language Research Unit," *Progress Report II, Annexe V,* Vol. 2, Cambridge University Press, Cambridge, England, 1956, pp. 26–38.

45. Mattingly, I. E., "Post-editing for Feedback," *Mathematical Linguistics and Automatic Translation* (Report No. NSF–3), The Computation Laboratory, Harvard University, Cambridge, Massachusetts, August, 1959, pp. I:1–26.

46. Micklesen, L. R., "Russian–English MT," *American Contributions to the Fourth International Congress of Slavicists, Moscow, September, 1958,* Mouton & Co., 's-Gravenhage, Netherlands, 1958.

47. Oswald, V. A., Jr., and S. L. Fletcher, "Proposals for the Mechanical Resolution of German Syntax Patterns," *Modern Language Forum,* Vol. 36, No. 3–4, 1951, pp. 81–104.

48. Oswald, V. A., Jr., and R. H. Lawson, "An Idioglossary for Mechanical Translation," *Modern Language Forum,* Vol. 38, No. 3–4, 1953, pp. 1–11.

49. Parker-Rhodes, A. F., "Some Recent Work on Thesauric and Interlingual Methods in Machine Translation." (Presented at the International Conference for Standards on a Common Language for Machine Searching and Translation, September 6–12, 1959, Cleveland, Ohio.)

50. Perry, J. W., "Translation of Russian Technical Literature by Machine; Notes on Preliminary Experiments," *Mechanical Translation,* Vol. 2, No. 1, July, 1955, pp. 15–24.

51. Reifler, Erwin, "The First Conference on Mechanical Translation," *Mechanical Translation,* Vol. 1, No. 2, August, 1954, pp. 23–32.

52. ———, "Mechanical Determination of the Constituents of German Substantive Compounds," *Mechanical Translation,* Vol. 2, No. 1, July, 1955, pp. 3–14.

53. ———, "Outline of the Project," *Linguistic and Engineering Studies in the Automatic Translation of Scientific Russian into English,* University of Washington Press, Seattle, Washington, June, 1958.

54. Reynolds, A. C., "The Conference on Mechanical Translation," *Mechanical Translation,* Vol. 1, No. 3, December, 1954, pp. 47–55.

55. Richens, R. H., "Interlingual Machine Translation," *Computer Journal,* Vol. 1, No. 3, October, 1958, pp. 144–147.

56. National Bureau of Standards, "Syntax Patterns in English Studied by Electronic Computer," *Computers and Automation,* Vol. 6, No. 7, 1957, pp. 15–17, 32.

57. Tasman, P., "Literary Data Processing," *IBM Journal of Research and Development,* Vol. 1, No. 3, July, 1957, pp. 249–256.

58. Thomas, R., "The Use of SEAC in Syntactic Analysis," *Report of the Eighth Annual Round Table Meeting on Linguistics and Language Studies,* Monograph Series on Language and Linguistics, No. 10, Georgetown University Press, Washington, D.C., 1957, pp. 151–161.

59. Toma, P., *SERNA System,* Georgetown University Press, Washington, D.C., June, 1959.

60. Wall, R., "Use of the IBM 650 Computer for the Study of Syntax in the Solution of the Problem of Multiple Meaning," *Linguistic and Engineering Studies in the Automatic Translation of Scientific Russian into English,* University of Washington Press, Seattle, Washington, June, 1958.

61. ———, and Udo K. Niehaus, "Russian to English Machine Translation with Simple Logical Processing," *Linguistic and Engineering Studies in the Automatic Translation of Scientific Russian into English,* University of Washington Press, Seattle, Washington, June, 1958. (Presented at the AIEE Fall General Meeting, Chicago, Illinois, October 7–11, 1957.)

62. Worth, D. S., "Linear Content," *Word,* Vol. 15, No. 1, April, 1959, pp. 183–191.

63. Yngve, V. H., "Sentence-for-Sentence Translation," *Mechanical Translation,* Vol. 2, No. 2, November, 1955, pp. 29–37.

64. ———, "A Framework for Syntactic Translation," *Mechanical Translation,* Vol. 4, No. 3, December, 1957, pp. 59–65.

65. ———, "A Programming Language for Mechanical Translation," *Mechanical Translation,* Vol. 5, No. 1, July, 1958, pp. 25–41.

66. ———, "A Model and an Hypothesis for Language Structure," *Proceedings of the American Philosophical Society,* Vol. 104, No. 5, 1960, pp. 444–466.

CHAPTER V

# The Application of
# Statistical Methods in
# Linguistic Research

## 1. Random Events and Statistical Regularities; the Concept of Statistical Rules

In studying language, we constantly encounter situations in which various language phenomena cannot be described fully and yet briefly. Language is a system composed of a large number of diverse objects interacting according to very complex laws. The functioning of linguistic units usually depends on so many factors that it is practically impossible to take them all into account and determine the outcome of their interaction. For this reason, it is only comparatively rarely that one can formulate strict, *fully determined* rules about language objects.

By rules that are fully determined, we mean assertions of the following type: Upon realization of a fully determined complex of conditions, a definite event *must* take place.

For example, in modern Russian, given "a voiced consonant at the end of a word before a pause," the consonant must become unvoiced.[1] This makes it possible to formulate fully de-

_____

[1] [For a discussion of this, see the *Grammatika russkogo yazyka* [*Grammar of the Russian Language*], Vol. I, Izd-vo AN SSSR, Moscow, 1960, pp. 73–75.— Tr.]

termined rules about a voiced consonant at the end of a word. Such simple cases are all too rare.

Thus, we encounter serious difficulties in attempting to formulate equally strict rules about the use of the article before a noun in modern English. To define the conditions for article choice universally and unambiguously, we must take many different factors into account. If we analyze the rules given in ordinary grammars, we are soon convinced that all of these more or less brief rules do not allow us to define uniquely the conditions for choosing an article. If we assume that errors occur when the rules do not embrace all possible conditions, then we can increase the number of factors to be accounted for. The number of errors will decrease, but since so many factors influence the choice of an article, and since their interaction is so complex, the rules will become more and more cumbersome. Here it does not matter how much we complicate the rules; we still cannot be sure that they will handle all cases correctly. Obviously, too, overcomplicated[2] rules are of little use either in the theoretical description of language or in a practical application.

In other words, we cannot make a sufficiently exhaustive list of interacting conditions that uniquely determine article choice, and so we must continue to make errors. The occurrence of errors when our rules are applied indicates that after fulfillment of the complex of conditions enumerated in the rules, a "substitution of a certain type of article" may or may not take place. Such an event is called *random* with respect to that complex of conditions.

However, when a certain event $A$ is random with respect to a given complex of conditions $S$, this does not mean that one cannot establish any connection between $A$ and $S$ in general. Specifically, even with the simultaneous occurrence of all conditions in set $S$, event $A$ may or may not occur; a certain regularity in the occurrence of $A$ is observable, given a high occurrence frequency for $S$; event $A$ has a definite *frequency*.[3]

For example, in applying the rules of article placement (pre-

---

[2] For example, the rules for choice of an article occupy 50 printed pages.

[3] By the frequency of $A$, we mean the ratio of the number of occurrences of event $A$ to the total number of times $A$ *might have* occurred—i.e., to the number of times the conditions $S$ occurred. The concept of frequency will be discussed in greater detail below.

sented in an authoritative English grammar) in order to translate a certain phrase from some language into English, we could well make some errors, such as would be shown by the nonoccurrence of $A$ (the choice of the proper article) in spite of the occurrence of $S$ (enumerated in the rules for the condition). However, if we apply these rules to a large body of text, we shall determine the article correctly in a significant number of cases, and if the rules have been formulated particularly well, such cases will be in the majority. Moreover, if we use these rules to translate several different texts of large volume containing an approximately equal number of cases in which article rules must be applied, we shall see that the number of instances of correct article determination will be about the same for each.

This means that although our rules are not fully determined, there is still a definite connection between the set of conditions enumerated in them and the realization of "correct article choice"; the connection is expressed quantitatively by the fact that correct choices are made with a definite frequency when the conditions occur frequently.

The regularity with which the random event $A$ occurs with a definite frequency, given frequent occurrence of the particular set of conditions $S$, is called *statistical*. Correspondingly, we call those rules *statistical* that contain the following kind of statement: Given frequent occurrence of a fully determined set of conditions $S$, event $A$ occurs with a definite frequency.

In other words, if we formulate rules about articles that will determine the article correctly not less than 80 per cent of the time, then we can call such rules statistical. We can show that a large number of linguistic situations exist that can be described both fully and briefly only by means of statistical rules.

For example, in order to avoid using the same noun twice in the same sentence or in two juxtaposed sentences, we may try substituting a third-person personal pronoun: *Stat'ya "N" posvyashchena analizu dannogo slovosochetaniya.* **Ona** *podrobno izlagaet* . . . [Article "N" is devoted to the analysis of a certain phrase. **It** (instead of *stat'ya* = article) describes in detail . . .].

There are, however, a significant number of instances in which such substitution is impossible, since various grammatical and syntactic peculiarities of a particular sentence cause ambiguity with respect to the antecedent of the pronoun: *Portret napisan izvestnym khudozhnikom; ya nedavno videl **ego*** [The portrait was painted by a famous artist; I saw it/him[4] recently]. Or: *Sestra vstupila v artisticheskuyu gruppu; **ona** uekhala na gastroli* [My sister joined an artistic group; she/it[5] went on the stage].

Individual instances of the impossibility of substitution have been given in textbooks on literary editing, but no one has yet succeeded in formulating strict, entirely specific rules covering all cases. This is apparently due to the fact that the reasons for this impossibility—conditions in which it must necessarily be the case that "substitution is impossible" ("the noun must be repeated")—are usually quite specific, and frequently depend on the individual peculiarities of a *particular* phrase. Any attempt to formulate entirely specific rules will lead to the necessity of listing all of these peculiarities, which is pointless. L. N. Iordanskaya (a co-worker in the Structural and Applied Linguistics Section, Institute of Linguistics, Academy of Sciences, U.S.S.R.), while studying this question in connection with machine translation, proposed statistical rules for replacement (or rather for determining the impossibility of substitution) of a noun with a third-person personal pronoun. Her approach is based on a deliberate refusal to enumerate the conditions under which "impossibility of substitution" must occur. She considered a large number of sentences in which corresponding conditions occurred, while "impossibility of substitution" may or may not have occurred. She then separated out the set of conditions that caused the most frequent occurrence of "impossibility of substitution." She succeeded in formulating compact statistical rules that pointed to the following result: "With frequent occurrence of some set of conditions, in no less than 94 per cent of the cases did 'impossibility of substitution' occur; i.e., the noun is to be repeated."

We emphasize the fact that although Iordanskaya's rules are not valid in every case, but only in the majority of cases, this

---

[4] [Both *portret* and *khudozhnikom* are masculine singular, while *ego* is ambiguously animate or inanimate and could refer to either noun.—Tr.]

[5] [Both *sestra* and *gruppu* are feminine singular, while *ona*—ambiguously animate or inanimate—could refer to either.—Tr.]

does not in the least decrease their value, because the attempt to formulate fully specified rules for this purpose (i.e., rules true for all cases without exception) has failed. Naturally, it is better to have such statistical rules as those already described, true no less than 94 per cent of the time, than to have no rules at all or to have ten pages of rules for each individual object of linguistic study.

The study of random events and of the statistical regularities to which they are subject is the province of special mathematical disciplines: probability theory and mathematical statistics. Accordingly, to the degree that certain phenomena in language can be considered as random, while the regularities connecting them with a definite set of conditions can be called statistical, the methods of probability theory and mathematical statistics must be applied in linguistics.

## 2. Method for Producing Statistical Rules; Evaluation of the Reliability of the Results of Observations

Linguists are well aware that a significant number (perhaps even the majority) of linguistic rules *formulated as if they were fully specified* are not so in fact, since cases are constantly arising in which an event does not occur in spite of the occurrence of the set of conditions indicated in the rules, even though it supposedly *had* to occur. For this reason, many assertions are made in linguistics that later turn out to be sometimes true, sometimes false in analogous conditions. We must make such assertions more accurate by indicating how frequently they are valid, i.e., by creating statistical rules.[6]

Since a statistical regularity connecting a set of conditions S with an event A is apparent only when S occurs frequently, it is evident that to formulate statistical rules we must make many observations of the co-occurrence frequency of A with S. In mathematical statistics, there are definite general methods by which such observations are to be made and frequencies calculated for the occurrence of random events.

---

[6] See [4], pp. 112–130, for example.

In general, linguists have long been occupied with calculations of the frequencies of various kinds of events—the appearance of certain phonemes, words, forms, constructions, etc. Here, in fact, the appearance of a certain form or word from among others in a text of a particular period or author should be looked upon as a random event, while the set of conditions with which a certain event is connected by statistical regularity extends to such concepts as "Russian texts of the seventeenth century," etc. Such calculations should also be made according to the rules of mathematical statistics. Yet, in the overwhelming majority of studies, these rules are not observed and, what is especially important, the results obtained are not accompanied by evaluations of their reliability.

The need to evaluate reliability is dictated by the following considerations. A linguist attempting to make some assertion about a linguistic fact cannot, as a rule, track down all the possible text ("*parole*") from a given period or ethnic group; the researcher is confined to studying a specific part of this whole—some collection of texts or sound recordings. And so one must judge whether an event occurs frequently (i.e., one must judge to what extent the occurrence of condition $S$ brings with it the occurrence of $A$) on the basis of a *limited number* of observations.

According to linguistic practice, the quantity of material being studied is usually limited to the amount required by the researcher. Having selected the quantity of text that he can handle, which he therefore considers sufficient, and having written an imposing number of cards—hundreds or even thousands—the author considers his material complete and begins to analyze and distribute it.

The results of this type of research usually lead to an assertion such as: "In the language of contemporary Russian literature . . . ," or "In sixteenth-century English. . . ." But the author will have studied only a small part of the total text comprising "contemporary Russian literature." Just how legitimate is such generalization of results, obtained from doubly limited material, to the entire "language of contemporary Russian literature"? If one cannot treat all relevant text but only some part of it, one must attempt to draw conclusions about the whole text from this sample. If, however, one must generalize from a part to the whole, then one ought to know just how closely the facts pertaining to a part actually correspond to what takes place in the whole. Naturally, absolute correspondence is impossible; the degree of correspondence can vary considerably, making the reliability of our conclusions about the totality extremely variable. Hence, the intelligent thing is to demand that the reliability of conclusions about a whole text generalized from a sample be indicated in each case. For example, if on the basis of a specific, limited number of observations an assertion is made that for every 100 times certain rules were applied, 85 instances of correct article choice occurred, then one must still indicate how reliable his assertion is; if another researcher takes another 100 cases (i.e., applies the rules to another text), the occurrence of "correct article choice" may amount not to 85 times but to 60.

According to mathematical statistics, the fact that only a part of a whole—a sample—is available for immediate observation does not prevent us from making quite adequate statements about the whole. However, this is possible only when certain requirements regarding sampling are fulfilled.

There exist in mathematical statistics special methods for evaluating the reliability of results and for determining how large a sample must be to guarantee a certain degree of reliability. We shall discuss one of the simpler methods later. Because of space limitations, certain concepts of mathematical statistics introduced below will not be explained in detail; we shall only refer to the relevant textbook sources.

### 3. The Concepts of Frequency, Selection, and Relative Error

Let us take the following problem. If in a contemporary Russian mathematics text two nouns occur together without a preposition, one noun governing the other, what will be the case of the dependent noun?

We know from the rules of Russian grammar that the case of the dependent:

(1) must not be nominative;

(2) must not be prepositional, since only constructions without prepositions are involved here;

(3) must not be accusative—such constructions have not been encountered in Russian grammar;

(4) is not determined by the case of the main noun.

On this basis, one can assert that if there is a construction involving two nouns in which one governs the other, then the dependent noun will be in the genitive, the dative, or the instrumental case. This assertion does not satisfy us, however, because it is so indefinite. We can try to make it more specific by asserting that one of the possible cases is encountered more frequently than the others. To make this explicit we must conduct an experiment that consists of making observations of text. In doing so, we recognize that the appearance of any of the three enumerated cases is an accidental event with respect to the set of conditions: "a construction of any two nouns without a preposition, where one noun governs the other." Given frequent occurrence of that set of conditions, it is necessary to state how frequently the random event occurs: "the appearance of a particular case." So there are three possible results:

(1) appearance of the genitive case (gen.),

(2) appearance of the dative case (dat.),

(3) appearance of the instrumental case (instr.).

We shall call the frequency of appearance of a given case the ratio of the number of times that case appears to the total number of times that it might appear, i.e., to the number of two-noun constructions without prepositions. Let us call the frequencies of occurrence of the corresponding cases $P_{gen}$, $P_{dat}$, and $P_{instr}$. Numerical determination of these frequencies will be the solution of the problem. In inspecting text, we suppose that these frequencies are constant for all relevant texts, i.e., that whatever mathematics text we select, the ratio of use of the genitive and other cases will be approximately the same.[7]

We already know that statistical regularities appear only with frequent occurrence of the conditions. But what do we

---

[7] This is a "statement of the statistical homogeneity of texts." In some cases, it is only true in the first approximation. In mathematical statistics, there are methods for proving the reliability of this statement for concrete instances [3].

mean by "frequent"? As we know, the number of observations is always limited and represents only a sample of the whole. What kind of sampling will guarantee us the "right" to base our judgment of the whole on it? With this phrasing of the question we must turn our attention to the following essential factors.

### 3.1. SIZE OF SAMPLE

The larger the sample (the more text is sampled), the less chance there will be that the frequency observed in it differs significantly from the frequencies present in all texts, which in our example comprise the whole of Russian mathematics literature. If in determining the frequencies of cases of the dependent noun we scan a sample of text containing about 100 cases of two-noun, prepositionless constructions, there will still be samples of text that happen to contain no instance of a particular case, as well as samples in which one case is encountered disproportionately often. In looking over larger samples of text containing, for example, about 500 noun constructions, we will not find such significant "clumps" and "cutoffs," since the influence of accidental factors is limited.

Let us designate the size of the sample by $N$, the frequency of some case (for example, the genitive) observed in the sample by $P^*_{gen}$, the frequency of the same case as occurring in the whole text by $P_{gen}$. Then we can say that as $N \to \infty$, the absolute value of the difference $P_{gen} - P^*_{gen}$ tends toward zero, i.e.,

$$\left| P_{gen} - P^*_{gen} \right| \to 0.$$

This means that as the size of the sample increases, the value of the frequency calculated on the basis of the sample approaches the value of the frequency existing in the entire body of text, i.e., the difference between these values approaches zero. The difference $P - P^*$ is called the *absolute error of measurement*.

In order to characterize the degree to which the frequency determined from the sample approaches the frequency in the whole text, it is more useful to consider not the absolute but the *relative* error, which is the ratio of this difference to the measured value of $P$, i.e., $(P - P^*)/P$. The fact is that the absolute error may be very small if the measured values of $P$ and $P^*$ themselves are small, but this difference may be very significant in comparison with $P$ and can greatly change the accuracy of the measurements. For example, if in measuring a line 100 mm in length we obtain an absolute error of 5 mm, and in measuring a line 10 mm long we obtain the same absolute error, then in the first case, the error amounts only to 0.05, while in the second, it amounts to 0.5 of the measured magnitude. Thus, the accuracy of measurement can only be represented by the value of the *relative error*.

The larger the sample, the more accurate the calculation obtained. But there arises a question regarding the meaning of the expression "accurate calculation." What degree of accuracy will suffice; what relative error can be allowed? There is no general answer to this question. The limits of permissible error arise from practical considerations. It seems reasonable to demand, for example, that even in the roughest estimates, the relative error $\delta$ should be less than 30 per cent of the measured magnitude:

$$\delta = \frac{|P - P^*|}{P} < 0.3.$$

With the need for a more exact evaluation, the value of $\delta$ can be set at 5 per cent, etc.

### 3.2. FREQUENCIES

Sometimes it is necessary to determine the frequency of some phenomenon with a specified accuracy, i.e., with a specified relative error.

For example: In order to determine the optimum arrangement of the keyboard of a specialized typewriter for printing mathematical text, one must determine the frequency of the letter $F$ in mathematics texts.[8] We know that the letter $F$ is quite rare in literature, but we can show that in mathematics it is more frequently encountered because of the occurrence of such words as *funktsiya* [function], *faktorial* [factorial], *koeffitsient* [coefficient], and *differentsial* [differential]. In a prac-

---

[8] [That is, the equivalent Cyrillic letter.—Tr.]

tical problem, δ can be set at 10 per cent of the proposed frequency of the *F*.

According to some preliminary experimental data, the letter *F* occurs about twice out of every 1,000 letters of Russian mathematics text. In studying samples of text about 1,000 letters long, we found that as a result of accidental circumstances *F* did not occur at all in the first sample, while it was encountered four times in the second; i.e., in the first sample, its frequency was seemingly zero, while in the second, it was 0.004. The frequency observed in the first sample was essentially different from that in the second, while they both differed from the primary data (the third sample). This was due to the fact that the accidental incidence of *F* in our first and second samples completely changed the result. In fact, the frequency of this letter is so small that for a small sample—1,000 letters—accidental factors were felt very strongly, and, therefore, the results of the three samples differed from one another by a great deal more than 10 per cent.

If we increase the volume of the sample so that the letter *F* occurs within it not just two to four times but twenty, then the random occurrence of one or two extra *F*'s in the sample will not change the result, since the action of random factors is greatly limited,[9] and the relative error of measurement will not go beyond the specified limits.

Obviously, in order to ascertain the frequency of the letter *U* (about two and one-half times as frequent as *F*) with the same relative error, we will find a considerably smaller sample satisfactory.

It follows from what has been said that for a given relative error δ, the smaller the frequency, the larger the sample needed:

$$\text{if } P \to 0, \quad \text{then } N \to \infty.$$

The interrelation between the frequency *P*, the sample *N*, and the relative error δ can be illustrated in an elementary statistical formula. This can be written in simplified form as

$$\delta = \frac{z_p\sqrt{1-P}}{\sqrt{NP}}, \tag{1}$$

---

[9] [This clause (beginning with "since") is a misrepresentation of probability theory.—Tr.]

where $\delta$ is the relative error, $N$ is the sample size, $P$ is the frequency, and $z_p$ is the constant (found in a special table usually presented in textbooks on probability theory). In the following discussion, $z_p$ will have the value 2.[10]

Using this formula, we can solve two basic problems that arise when a linguist attempts to make a quantitative evaluation. These problems are:

(1) Evaluation of the reliability of results, i.e., determination of the relative error with which the frequency of some phenomenon is calculated from a particular sample.

(2) Determination of the sample size that will guarantee the calculation of the frequency of some phenomenon with a specified relative error.

Let us consider the first problem. Its "physical meaning" was presented above, and we already know that given a large sample for a particular, defined frequency, we can expect better, more reliable results.

For example: In Spanish, there is widespread alternation in verbal roots: About forty kinds of alternation have been counted (e.g., *sentir—siente, sentir—sintió, saber—supo*). But not all forms with alternation are used equally often in texts. To perfect a methodology for teaching Spanish and for several other purposes, it is important to know which types of alternation are basic from the standpoint of the frequency with which they are encountered in texts. In order to be able to use the results, we must be sure of their reliability. To be considered reliable, conclusions about the frequency of forms with a certain type of alternation must be obtained with a relative error of less than

---

[10] $z_p = 2$ corresponds to the confidence level $p = 0.95$. Some elucidation of the content of the concept of "confidence levels" is given below. For more details on this, see [3]. Here and in what follows, frequencies are represented as being distributed according to Gauss' law [the "normal" distribution—Tr.] (see [3] and [29]).

[We have corrected formula (1), given incorrectly in the original text. Since $P$ is a number that cannot be known but only estimated, it is important to realize that this formula is approximately valid for large samples when the estimate $P^*$ is used instead of $P$. The proper interpretation of the formula is the following: The probability is $p$ (say, 0.95) that an estimate $P^*$, based on a sample of $N$ observations, will have a relative error $(|P^* - P|)/P$ less than $\delta$ as calculated by formula (1). Cf. Alexander M. Mood, *Introduction to the Theory of Statistics*, McGraw-Hill Book Co., Inc., New York, 1950, pp. 220–222 and 236.–Tr.]

10 per cent. Our samples will obviously be all forms of irregular verbs encountered in text. We shall then determine the frequency of each type of alternation; the number of forms with a particular type of alternation will be compared with the total number of forms of irregular verbs in the text under investigation. For the sake of simplicity, we shall confine our example to four types of alternation that are usually given first in teaching irregular verbs, relegating the other types to a conditional fifth type. Having determined the frequency of each type, we shall calculate from formula (1) the error with which these frequencies were calculated. The results of the observations are shown in Table 1.

In column 3 of Table 1, the frequency of each type is written

TABLE 1

| 1 | 2 | 3 | 4 |
|---|---|---|---|
| Alternation-type number | Characteristics of alternation | Frequency of alternation type | Relative error |
| I | *e/ie*<br>*sentir—siente* | $\dfrac{655}{1721} \sim 0.38$ | $\pm 7.8\%$ |
| II | *o/ue*<br>*morir—muere* | $\dfrac{495}{1721} \sim 0.29$ | $\pm 9.04\%$ |
| III | *e/i*<br>*pedir—pido* | $\dfrac{83}{1721} \sim 0.05$ | $\pm 22\%$ |
| IV | no letter/*y*<br>*construir—construye* | $\dfrac{87}{1721} \sim 0.05$ | $\pm 21\%$ |
| V | All others | $\dfrac{401}{1721} \sim 0.23$ | $\pm 10\%$ |

The total number of irregular-verb forms is 1721.

as a proper fraction, namely, the ratio of the number of occurrences of the "appearance of a certain type of alternation" (i.e., good results) to the number of possible occurrences (i.e., to the number of forms with alternations in the text being studied): Type I was encountered 655 times, II—495 times, III—83 times, IV—87 times, and V (conditional)—401 times. In all, $655 + 495 + 83 + 87 + 401 = 1,721$ forms with alternations occurred in the text (1,721 possible occurrences). For clarity, the frequency of each type is shown in decimals, as well. For example, the frequency of type I is 0.38. This means that for each 100 forms with alternation, *about* 38 forms had type I alternation. For reasons already stated, the sample-determined frequency is only approximate. The relative error, in column 4, shows the *limits* of this approximation, to wit: If the frequency 0.38 is determined with a relative error of ± 7.8 per cent, this means that in scanning any Spanish text, we shall find, for every 100 forms of verbs with alternation, from [38 − .078 (38)] to [38 + .078 (38)] forms of type I. Since .078 (38) is approximately equal to 3,[11] this means that the number of type I forms will oscillate from 35 to 41 for every 100 occurrences of forms with alternation.[12]

According to mathematical statistics, there can also be instances in which for every 100 forms with alternation, type I occurs less than 35 times (we shall call this number the lower limit of frequency) or more than 41 times (the upper limit); however, such large deviations will be encountered only very rarely.

The constant $z_p$ in the formula for determining the relative error defines the number of occurrences of such large deviations which go beyond the lower and upper limits. In particular, the value we chose for the constant, $z_p = 2$, corresponds to $p = 0.95$, which means that in 95 out of 100 samples, type I frequency will oscillate (for each 100 verbal forms with alternation) within the indicated bounds, which it can exceed in only 5 samples.[13]

---

[11] The number of occurrences is not expressed as a fraction.

[12] [Or rather, from 35 per cent to 41 per cent in samples of 1,721 occurrences of forms with alternation.—Tr.]

[13] [That is, in 95 out of 100 samples of 1,721 occurrences.—Tr.]

Comparing the values of relative error written in column 4, we note that not all the results are equally precise. For example, the accuracy with which the type III frequency was determined is clearly not sufficient according to the accepted criterion. This happens in a sample of fixed size because a smaller frequency (and type III, obviously, occurs more rarely) will cause a greater relative error. Consequently, if one is to obtain results for type III as accurate as those for type I, one must enlarge the sample.

We come, thus, to the second problem: determination of the sample size that will guarantee a specific accuracy. According to the accepted criterion, the relative error may not exceed 0.1. The frequency of type III is $P = 83/1,721 \sim 0.05$. It has a relative error of $\pm 22$ per cent. We have thus found that for each 1,000 forms with alternation, there will occur approximately 38 to 58 forms of type III. In producing the sample, we cannot know beforehand how many times the form being sought occurs in it, but we can foresee that the required accuracy of 10 per cent will be guaranteed even if a minimal number of type III forms, corresponding to the lower limit, is found in a given concrete sample. Thus, in determining the size of the sample, we will exceed the lower bound of the frequency of type III; according to (1):

$$0.1 = \frac{2}{\sqrt{0.038N}}, \qquad \text{whence } N = 10,500;$$

i.e., in order to define the frequency of type III with an accuracy of not less than $\pm 10$ per cent, one must scan a text containing not less than 10,500 forms with alternations.

It is exactly the same in determining the frequency of the letter $F$ (see pp. 89-90) with the same relative error as for $U$; one must take a much larger sample for $F$ than for $U$.[14]

In connection with what has already been said, we must now turn our attention to one mistake commonly made by linguists in formulating their problems. The question is usually posed: We want to find the frequency of a certain form (phoneme, word, etc.); how do we calculate the size of the sample needed?

---

[14] [The Cyrillic letter transliterated by $U$ is common; that transliterated by $F$ is rare.—Tr.]

It was emphasized earlier that the concept "necessary size of the sample" has no meaning if one has not defined the degree of accuracy to be guaranteed. But in order to use formula (1) one must know with what approximate frequency to begin one's calculations; otherwise, there will be two unknowns in the formula. This also has an inclusive aspect: Given an equal specified error, in order to determine the least frequency, one must take a larger sample. But it is this very determination of the frequency that is the goal of the study. The way out of this difficulty is through a preliminary experiment.[15]

The preliminary experiment can be conducted as follows. From a small sample, one determines the frequency of the event being studied, with a certain relative error. Then, exceeding the lower limit of frequency (pp. 93-94) and of the relative error permissible for final results, one calculates the necessary size of the sample.

Take, for example, the determination of the frequency of type III alternation in the root of the Spanish verb. We can consider the calculation in Table 1 for type III to be the preliminary experiment; initially, in a sample containing 1,721 forms with alternation, the frequency of type III, the error, and the lower limit of frequency were established. Then, from the lower limit of frequency and the *required* accuracy, the necessary size of the sample was found to be 10,500.

We have discussed here some of the simplest methods of treating the results of observations with regard to evaluating their reliability.

Linguistic studies have appeared recently that apply methods developed in mathematical statistics for the design of experiments and evaluation of reliability. In this connection, Yule's book, *The Statistical Study of Literary Vocabulary* [48], B. Epstein's introductory article in Josselson's frequency glossary [29], articles by American psychologists in the anthology *Studies in Language Behavior* [39], and several other papers—[4], [34], and [35]—are all very interesting.

---

[15] In some cases, the numerical bounds of the frequencies we want to obtain in the course of the study can be evaluated on the basis of data already existing in the literature.

## 4. A Statistical Approach to the Description of Individual Linguistic Phenomena

A statistical approach to the description of individual linguistic phenomena is not something new. The first statistical studies of lexicology appeared at the end of the last century. From then on, a large volume of literature has accumulated, primarily on the statistics of words and sounds (or phonemes)—[4], [13], [18], [26], [40], [41], [44], etc.

Certain of the methods used in these studies excite one's attention, but the most interesting studies generally contain a complex mathematical apparatus, which is not available to linguists. Therefore, it seems useful in the present short work to turn our attention to the *essence* of the statistical approach in the studies mentioned, at the same time reducing the mathematical apparatus to a minimum.

We shall pay particular attention to (1) attempts to describe lexicology statistically; (2) studies of the composition of words, with respect to the number of syllables; (3) research using statistical methods to study the rhythmic structure of poetry.

### 4.1. STATISTICAL METHODS IN LEXICOLOGICAL RESEARCH[16]

The first attempts to apply statistical methods in describing the facts of language are connected with the compilation of so-called "frequency dictionaries" (the first we know of is Kaeding's dictionary [30], published in 1898).

A frequency dictionary is a list of words (a vocabulary) in which every word carries an indication of its occurrence frequency in a text of a certain length. For example, Kaeding studied texts with a total length of 11 million words, and then vocabularized them and counted the frequency of each word throughout the 11 million running words. Frequency dictionaries permit one to compare words from the standpoint of their usage frequency; hence, their sphere of application is rather

---

[16] Here and in what follows, "lexicology" and "dictionary" refer to the dictionary form of a text, a vocabulary. The lexical structure of an individual word and the system of its meanings are not considered.

large. The data of frequency dictionaries are of great theoretical interest for studies of certain properties of text with regard to its relation to the vocabulary and to the frequencies of words composing a given text.

Let us go into this a little further.

(a) *The statistical structure of text.*

Suppose we have a certain text $N$ words in length and its list of (different) words $L$ in which $N > 1$ and $L > 1$. Detaching ourselves from the properties of real text, we can imagine that the following relations exist between wordlist and text:

(1) $N = L$ (all the words in the text are different);
(2) $N > L$ (some of the words are repeated).

Most real text corresponds to the second type. If we fix the value of $N$ (say, $N = 10,000$), then we cannot say anything about $L$ beforehand, other than the fact that it is less than 10,000.[17] If we fix the value of $N$ and the value of $L$—say, $N = 10,000$ and $L = 2,000$—then several quite distinct situations are theoretically possible. For example:

Text 1. 1,500 words in wordlist $L$ occur once, accounting for 1,500 occurrences, while the other 8,500 words of the text consist of repetitions of 500 words in the list.

Text 2. 50 words from list $L$ occur once, and 9,950 text words are repetitions of 1,950 words in the list, etc.

This means that the "structure" of the text, from the standpoint of word-repetition, is still not defined either by the length of the text or by the size of the wordlist but, rather, by the number of individual groups of words repeated a specific number of times. In order to describe the structure of text 1, it is clearly essential to show not only that there are words in it occurring only once, because there are also such words in text 2, but also that the number of words in the group with text-frequency 1 is 1,500, while this group in text 2 is thirty times smaller.

Suppose we describe the "structure" of the text from the standpoint of word repetition, showing how many words have frequency 1, 2, etc. We are not dealing here with individual

---

[17] We shall deal later with the question of how the size of the wordlist $L$ is related to the length of text $N$.

properties of words,[18] and we extract only that property which is important for characterizing text from a particular standpoint.

Since we know that text 1 contains 1,500 words with a frequency of 1, and text 2 has only 50 such words, we can assert that the chance of randomly selecting from the text one word with a frequency of 1 (or, to put it another way, the probability of a word with frequency 1) is thirty times greater for text 1 than it is for text 2.

We shall call the "structure" of the text, in the sense indicated above, its "statistical structure." We shall consider that the statistical structure of the text is known if, for any possible frequency of a word, the probability of randomly selecting from text a word with the given frequency is known.

The "possible" frequency (i.e., the scale of values for the frequency of a word) is defined by the fact that a word cannot have frequency 0 (we are considering only words actually encountered in a given text); and since $L > 1$ and $L < N$ (see p. 97), the word cannot have the frequency $N$, for this would mean that the text consisted of repetitions of one single word. Thus, a word's frequency (we shall call it $\xi$) can take any integer value within the interval $1 \leq \xi \leq N$.

The chance of randomly selecting from the text[19] a word having a particular frequency depends on what *proportion* of words with a given frequency exists among the other text words. To find the probability of randomly selecting from text[20] a word with $\xi = 1$, one must divide the number of words with $\xi = 1$ (there are 1,500 of them) by the text length[21] (10,000). We write this as follows:

$$P\{\xi = 1\} = \frac{1,500}{10,000} = 0.15.$$

---

[18] We are assuming that we know for sure what words to call *individual,* and which to consider *different.*

[19] [The author should have said "from the wordlist."—Tr.]

[20] [From the wordlist.—Tr.]

[21] [By the length of the wordlist, which in this case is $L = 2,000$. To estimate the probability of selecting from *text* a word that occurs $\xi$ times, multiply $\xi$ by the number of words in the wordlist that occur $\xi$ times (say, $L_\xi$) and divide by $N$: $P\{\xi = 1\} = \xi L_\xi / N$. In the example, $\xi = 1$ and $L_\xi = 1,500$, hence $P\{\xi = 1\} = (1)(1,500)/10,000 = 0.15$. But take $\xi = 2$ and $L_\xi = 500$; then $P\{\xi = 2\} = (2)(500)/10,000 = 0.10$, and the formula in the text is incorrect.—Tr.]

We write the probability of selection of words with frequencies 2, 3, etc., in the same way. After we have calculated all of these probabilities, we can say that we know the statistical structure of the text, or, to put it another way, the distribution of probabilities with which the random variable "frequency of a word" takes some value or another.

If we pursue the procedure described here, using the information about word frequency presented in frequency dictionaries, and compare the statistical structures (distributions of probabilities) obtained for various languages, then it turns out that they are *extremely similar.* The general aspect of the probability distribution obtained can be expressed graphically as follows: We take a system of rectilinear coordinates, and plot on the *x*-axis the scale of values for the frequency $\xi$ of a word. On the *y*-axis, we plot the probability $P$ with which a word's frequency takes a certain value. (Working with one text, we need not always divide the number of words with a particular frequency by the length of the text,[22] but can merely plot the number of words with a given frequency directly along the *y*-axis.) Joining these points, we obtain a curve having approximately the form presented in Figure 3.[23]

Experiments show that such graphs, drawn from material on any language, have common features:[24]

1. The curve showing word frequency as a function of occurrence frequency has one peak (the maximum point), located at $\xi = 1$. This obviously means that in any sufficiently large text there are more words having frequency 1 than words having frequencies of 2 or 20.

2. After $\xi = 1$, a sharp decrease in probability occurs, causing the highest possible value for $\xi$ to correspond usually to $y = 1$; this means that in any one text there is only one *most frequent* word. We can conclude from this that not every theoretically constructed statistical structure for text (see p. 97) corresponds to real texts. For example, no texts have been observed

---

[22] [By the length of the wordlist.—Tr.]

[23] Such a graph is sometimes called a Yule distribution [48].

[24] We note with interest that if we do not study all the words in a text, but only nouns or only verbs, the graph (or a table corresponding to it) has *generally* the same character.

up to now for which the probability distribution curve has more than one peak, or a peak such that $\xi > 1$, etc.

We can assume that since the *general* features described are inherent in the statistical structures of various texts in various languages, they are connected with some peculiarities of the functioning of language as such, and are not connected with the "language of Pushkin" as opposed to the "language of Tolstoy," or with the English language as opposed to French.

A detailed study of the statistical structures of various texts reveals that, aside from the general, similar features already

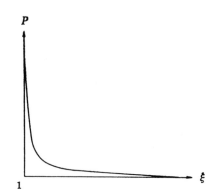

FIGURE 3.   The Probability $P$ with Which a Word's Frequency Takes a Certain Value as a Function of the Frequency $\xi$.

described, there are also essential differences among texts from the standpoint of frequency of word distribution. This becomes evident, for example, when one compares the statistical structures of the texts of various authors writing in one language (Figure 4).

Curves I and II (Figure 4), which describe word distribution for the works of various authors, have the general features shown in Figure 3 but, at the same time, they are quite different from each other; e.g., in text I, there are more low-frequency words (1, 2, 3) than in text II, and fewer words of very high frequency, i.e., there are more *different* words and fewer repetitions.

In this sense, one can say that the wordlist for text I is more varied than that for text II, or that for someone studying this foreign language, it will be easier to read II, etc.; in general, one can make several comprehensive judgments about each of these texts, basing them on the nature of their statistical structure.

We note that in linguistics one often speaks of the "wealth" of a vocabulary, or of its "homogeneity," about a similarity or a difference in the styles of various texts or authors, basing such remarks primarily on intuitive feelings, and sometimes accompanying them with statements that certain words or forms are encountered "more often" or "less frequently" in author $A$'s

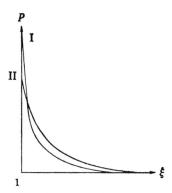

FIGURE 4. Word Distributions for Works of Different Writers. (In text I, there are more low-frequency words and fewer high-frequency words than in text II.)

works than in those of author $B$. Comparative study of statistical structures sharpens such subjective remarks to greater accuracy, and allows one to introduce exact measurements for such characteristics as wealth of vocabulary, and the similarity or difference between texts from the standpoint of the use of specific word classes, such as archaic, neutral, stylistically colored, or dialect words.

Since the concept of "style" presupposes the presence of several properties inherent in a given text (or texts) or author, as opposed to others—i.e., because it is based on a comparison and presentation of the similar and the different—it is reasonable to propose that style is *the sum of statistical characteristics describing the content properties of a particular text as distinct from others.*

For example, for describing the characteristic of vocabulary "wealth," we naturally choose characteristics uniquely defining curve I as differing from curve II, or defining the form of II as opposed to any other, etc. Such a method was applied successfully in the book of the famous English statistician G. U. Yule, *The Statistical Study of Literary Vocabulary* [48], in which one may familiarize himself completely with the essential numerical characteristics already discussed.

It is especially interesting to compare the statistical structures of texts in determining the authorship of anonymous works (provided we are already familiar with a certain amount of text known to be from the pen of the author supposed to have written the anonymous material).

The methodology of a detailed study has the following general features:

(1) A graph (or table) showing the word distribution of the anonymous work is drawn (Yule studied only noun distribution; it might have been more effective to tabulate other unambiguous parts of speech as well).

(2) Analogous tables are made for texts by two (or more) authors supposed to have written the anonymous text.

(3) For each table (anonymous text, author I, author II, etc.), numerical characteristics are collected, describing in sufficient detail the differences among the distributions in the different texts. Then these numerical characteristics are compared, and if those of the anonymous text more closely resemble those of author II than of I, we have reason to conclude that the anonymous text is by author II.

(b) *The relation between text length and the size of the wordlist.*

One aspect of the relationship between texts and wordlists is the relation between text length (measured in words[25]) and length of wordlist. We have already observed that even if we know the text length, $N$, we still cannot say anything about the size of the wordlist, $L$.

Of course, one can be sure a priori that in a novel 200 pages

---

[25] The formulation of the question does not depend on the definition of "word"; text length could even be measured by the number of printed characters.

long there are more different words than in a three-page story, but experiment has shown that 100 pages of the novel contain more than half as many different words as the whole novel. On the other hand, equally long works by different authors often differ greatly in wordlist length; sometimes a shorter text by one author has a broader vocabulary than a longer one by another.

Apparently, one cannot obtain through logical discussion an answer to questions regarding the general character of the connection between $L$ and $N$. However, for any concrete text, one can construct a graph (see Figure 5) of the function $L = F(N)$. (This is read "$L$ is a certain function of $N$.") Here, the

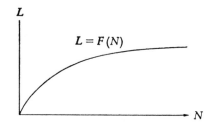

FIGURE 5.   Length $L$ of Wordlist as Function of Length $N$ of Text.

length of a text in words is plotted along the x-axis, and the number of different words used in it is plotted along y. We shall then obtain a dotted line joining the plotted points that closely approximates the curve shown in the graph. The nature of the connection between $L$ and $N$ was studied by Chotlos in school publications of American youth [39], by W. Kuraszkiewicz in Polish literary texts of the 16th century [31], and by Garcia Hoz in various texts of Spanish literary and commercial prose [22].

Experiments have shown that the graphs for $L = F(N)$ have several features in common, apparently not dependent upon the author's language or the character of the text. With increase in text length, the rate of increase of $L$ decreases; the curve always has a parabolic form, convex above. On the basis of these observations, attempts have been made to obtain an empirical formula for $L = F(N)$ that is generally applicable to all texts.

Carroll proposed an empirical formula having the form:

$$L = \frac{N}{k} (0.423 + k - \ln N + \ln k),$$

where $L$ is the number of different words, $N$ is the text-length, and $k$ is an empirical constant.[26]

If Carroll's formula were true for every text or for some particular group of texts, then for any text once one had found the value of $k$, one could always determine $L$, given $N$, and conversely.

But Chotlos (in [39]) has shown that this formula is erroneous. He proposed another empirical formula:

$$L = \frac{N(a - \ln N)}{b},$$

where $a$ and $b$ are empirical constants. In Chotlos' experiment, where $a = 11{,}670$ and $b = 11{,}268$, this formula describes the curve for increase in new words for $N < 18{,}000$ nicely; but the proof for this formula shows that when $N > 18{,}000$, it is unsatisfactory.

The attempts of Kuraszkiewicz to obtain a function for $L = F(N)$ were no more successful for comparing the vocabularies of various authors with respect to text-length. Thus, although this function can be given for each concrete text in a graph or table, an analytic description has not yet been found even for concrete texts. Moreover, we do not know whether a general analytic function exists for expressing the connection between wordlist and text.

(c) *Determination of the connection between a word's frequency and its rank by decreasing frequency ("Zipf's law").*

In linguistic literature much attention has been devoted to the study of a relation known as "Zipf's law" ( [15], [25], [33], [42], [49] ). The "law" itself, formulated before Zipf by J. B. Estoup [19] in 1916 and by E. U. Condon [17] in 1928, is as follows. Let us imagine a text $N$ words long to which is attached a wordlist $L$ words long, with an indication on every word of text-occurrence frequency. The words in the list are distributed

---

[26] Expanded in Chotlos' paper in [39].

in order of decreasing frequency and are renumbered from 1 (the number of the most frequent word) to $L$. We shall designate a word's frequency by $P_i$, and its rank by $r_i$, where $i$ can assume any integral value in the interval $1 \leq i \leq L$. The text's wordlist has the form:

| $r_i$ | $P_i$ |
|---|---|
| 1 | $P_1$ |
| 2 | $P_2$ |
| . | . |
| . | . |
| . | . |
| $r$ | $P_r$ |
| . | . |
| . | . |
| . | . |
| $L$ | $P_L$ |

Let us imagine that each of the $N$ words in the text is marked with a number $r_i$ corresponding to the location of the word in this wordlist. Then the most frequent (with frequency $P_1$) in the text will be found first [on the list—Tr.], a somewhat less frequent one (with frequency $P_2$) will be second, etc. Zipf's law, in defining the connection between a word's frequency and its rank in a list ordered on decreasing frequency, allows us to approximate the proportion of words with a given rank, or—to put it somewhat differently—to approximate the probability of a randomly selected word's having a certain rank.

We can write the formula for Zipf's law[27] in the following general form:

$$P\{r = i\} = kr^{-\gamma},$$

where $r$ is the rank of a word; $P$ is the probability that this word has a rank equal to $i$ (i.e., $P$ is the frequency of the $i$th word); $k$ and $\gamma$ are the empirically defined constants, approximately valid, in general, for all ordinary texts in European languages.

Essentially, Zipf's law assumes that once one has determined

---

[27] Zipf's law is introduced here in a form made precise by subsequent research (see [15] and [33]).

the constants $k$ and $\gamma$, one can calculate the frequency of a word from its rank (and conversely) by using the formula, and can also solve various problems for which one must know ranks and corresponding frequencies.

Thus, if it is always possible to find a word's frequency, $P_1$, $P_2, \ldots, P_m$, then it is always possible to find the total frequency of the $m$ most frequent words, i.e., the percentage of text covered by a certain number of the most frequent words:

$$\sum_{r=1}^{m} P_r = \sum_{r=1}^{m} kr^{-\gamma}.$$

If we assume that $k = 0.1$, $\gamma = 1.01$, and $m = 1,100$, then we obtain $\Sigma_{r=1}^{m} P_r = 0.8$, i.e., the 1,100 most frequently used words constitute 80 per cent of the text occurrences. We can show several other problems whose solutions are based on the application of Zipf's formula ( [10], [39] ). The unsatisfactory aspect of Zipf's relation consists in the fact that the constants $k$ and $\gamma$ are far from being as "general" as Zipf asserted. But this is too specific a question, and we shall not discuss it here.

## 4.2. WORD-DISTRIBUTION BY NUMBER OF SYLLABLES IN VARIOUS LANGUAGES

For many languages, the number of syllables in a randomly selected word is a random variable; there are one-, two-, three-syllable words, etc. One can assert that in texts in any given language, there is a preponderance of words with a particular number of syllables; for example, there are approximately twice as many bisyllabic as monosyllabic words in language $A$, and as many three- as four-syllable words, etc., while another ratio exists in language $B$, and so on.

The Soviet scientist S. G. Chebanov [12] (in 1947) and the German mathematician W. Fuchs [11] (in 1956) found that the distribution of words by the number of syllables in various languages is subject to a certain general regularity. We shall present here the main idea behind the discussions in Fuchs' paper [11], since it is the more interesting one to linguists from the standpoint of methodology.

In scanning concrete texts in English and Latin, Fuchs found that word distribution by number of syllables is very close for

various texts in one language, i.e., individual differences between authors writing in the same language are insignificant;
but for different languages, the data are quite different.

These differences can be illustrated as in the graph in Figure
6. The number of syllables possible in each word in a given

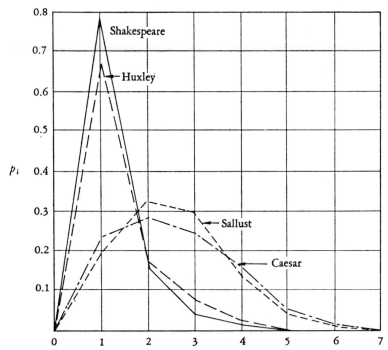

FIGURE 6. Number of Words of *i* Syllables as a Percentage
of the Total Number of Words in Text.

language is plotted along the *x*-axis. The number of words having a certain number of syllables is plotted along *y,* as a percentage of the total number of words in the text, i.e., the probability of a randomly selected word from the text being monosyllabic, bisyllabic, trisyllabic, etc. For example, the curve for
Shakespeare shows that about 80 per cent of the words in the text
are monosyllabic, and less than 20 per cent are bisyllabic; the
curve for Sallust shows that the largest group of words—about
32 per cent—is bisyllabic, with somewhat fewer trisyllabic, etc.
It is quite apparent how closely similar are the probability-dis-

tribution curves for various authors of English texts, and how much the curves for Caesar's and Sallust's texts differ from them.

However, the curves for various languages had other features in common, as well. The character of the experimentally obtained curves has allowed the author, building on certain statements in probability theory, to present the hypothesis that in all languages studied, word distribution by syllables follows a definite, general law. On the basis of this hypothesis, Fuchs obtained an analytic expression by means of which one can calculate, knowing only the average number of syllables in words in a given language, what percentage of the text is monosyllabic, bisyllabic, or other:

$$p_i = \frac{e^{-(\bar{\imath}-1)}(\bar{\imath} - 1)^{i-1}}{(i - 1)!}.$$

Here, $i$ is the number of syllables in a word; $\bar{\imath}$ is the average number of syllables per word for a certain language; $e$ is a constant (the base of natural logarithms) equal to 2.718 . . . ; $p_i$ is the percentage of $i$-complex words in the text, i.e., the probability that a word randomly selected from text in a particular language has $i$ syllables.

Let us take an example. In order to know the proportion of $i$-complex ($i = 1, 2, 3, \ldots$) words in Russian text, according to Fuchs, it is enough to know only one parameter: the average value of the number of syllables per word. This is calculated by a very simple experiment: For every word of a certain text, the number of syllables is written, and these figures are put together and the sum divided by the total number of words in the text.[28] For Russian, the average number of syllables is 2.228 (Fuchs' data). Then, in order to find, for example, the proportion of five-syllable words in Russian text, we substitute the corresponding values in Fuchs' formula. Thus:

$$p\{i = 5\} = \frac{2.718^{-(2.228-1)}(2.228 - 1)^4}{4!} = 0.0358.$$

This means that in Russian text, 3.58 per cent of the words have five syllables.

---

[28] One must bear in mind that in order to obtain sufficiently precise data, it is necessary to study a considerable amount of text (see above regarding this).

A comparison of the data obtained by calculations from the text and the formula yields good results.

A condition for the application of Fuchs' formula is the determination of the mean number of syllables per word for each language specified. But this does not lessen the practical value of the formula in the least, since calculation of the average number of syllables is incomparably less laborious than calculation of the entire distribution of words by number of syllables for various languages. In addition, the analytic relationship facilitates a comparative analysis of word distribution by syllables in various languages.

### 4.3. APPLICATION OF STATISTICAL METHODS FOR STUDYING THE STRUCTURE OF POETRY

Attempts to apply statistical methods to a study of the structure of poetry have already been made by Andrej Belyj [2]. The studies of the famous Soviet linguist and textologist B. V. Tomashevsky remain an unsurpassable example of this, as collected in his book *Poetry* [9]. In order to acquaint the reader with the methodology of Tomashevsky's statistical research, we shall present here several constructions from his paper on *The Iambic Pentameter of Pushkin*.

As is known, iambic verse, especially that of Pushkin, can have a very widely varied rhythmical structure, determined to a high degree by the distribution of pyrrhic feet—pairs of syllables without stress. For example, in iambic pentameter, in addition to the canonical type, such as

*Gorit vostok zareyu novoj,*
ᴗ ′/ ᴗ ′/ ᴗ ′/ᴗ ′/ᴗ

the most diverse variants are encountered: with the pyrrhic for the first foot, as in

*Ne dokuchal moral'yu strogoj,*
ᴗ ᴗ/ᴗ ′/ ᴗ ′/ ᴗ ′/ᴗ

or with the pyrrhic for the second and third feet, as in

*I klanyalsya neprinuzhdenno,*
ᴗ ′/ ᴗ ᴗ/ ᴗ ᴗ/ᴗ ′/ ᴗ

and others.

The greater the number of feet in the iambic line, the more possibilities there are for combining pyrrhic feet with other kinds of feet. The only distinct syllable with a firmly fixed stress is the ultimate syllable, since it is the rhyming one.

In attempting to give a general description of the peculiarities of the iambs of Pushkin, B. V. Tomashevsky conducted broad statistical research, from which he found that between the *number of feet* (pairs of syllables) *in the line (x) and the average number of pyrrhic feet per line of poetry (y) there exists a fully determined strict relationship:*

$$y = 0.28(x - 1).$$

This means that each hundred lines of iambic tetrameter will contain an average of 100 (0.28) (4 − 1) pyrrhic feet, while each 100 lines of iambic pentameter will contain 100(0.28) (5 − 1) pyrrhic feet, etc.; i.e., the number of pyrrhic feet is proportional to the number of feet per line, minus the rhyming syllable, since the latter does not participate in the distribution of pyrrhic feet.

The formula $y = 0.28 (x - 1)$ agrees well with the experimental data for iambic di-, tetra-, penta-, and hexameter, and only slightly less well with trimeter.

But the rhythmic variety of iambic lines of more than two feet is determined not only by the number of pyrrhics but also by their location, i.e., where they occur in the line. Thus, in iambic trimeter one finds lines without pyrrhics, lines with a pyrrhic foot at the first foot (the first pair of syllables), with a pyrrhic for the second foot (the second pair of syllables), and with two pyrrhic feet—on the first and second pairs of syllables. Therefore, it seems reasonable to describe the iambic trimeter of a certain poet by indicating how frequently the corresponding line forms are encountered—in other words, on the basis of a statistical approach.

For example, the rhythmic structure of Pushkin's iambic trimeter may be characterized in the following manner.

For each 100 lines of iambic trimeter, there are 300 distinct feet that *could* be stressed, 100 of which are rhyming; as we have already said, these are always stressed. This means that 200 feet participate in the distribution of pyrrhics. There are, then, 200 possible *places*. Using B. V. Tomashevsky's formula, we can calculate how many of these will have pyrrhic feet: $y =$

$100(0.28) (3 - 1) = 56$. Thus, out of 200 places, 56 are pyrrhic, and the others are stressed. It remains to be determined at which places they occur. One cannot tell this a priori. Tomashevsky's statistical research has shown that out of 144 stresses falling on the first and second feet, about 40 occurred on the second foot, and the others on the first. This means that most lines have the pyrrhic for the second foot, while lines with a pyrrhic for the first foot, or with two pyrrhic feet, are quite rare.[29]

We will now cite several more complex discussions, in which the methods of probability theory are applied in studying the rhythmic structure of iambic caesural pentameter.

Iambic caesural pentameter is divided by the caesura into two half-verses, the first being like iambic dimeter, the second like trimeter. Can one deduce the regularities of distribution of pyrrhic feet for iambic caesural pentameter from the regularities for dimeter and trimeter? Or does iambic pentameter have its own unique structure?

We shall consider the first half-verse (see Table 2, column 1). Obviously, it cannot be equated with iambic dimeter, since the latter cannot have the pyrrhic for the second foot (the rhyming one), whereas in the first half-verse of iambic pentameter, there is nothing to stop the pyrrhic from being the second foot.

Since the form ⌣⌣/⌣⌣/ is impossible for the first half-verse, because by the rules of poetry at least one stressed word precedes the caesura, the following three types occur for the first half-verse:

> (1) ⌣′/ ⌣′/      (2) ⌣⌣/ ⌣′/      (3) ⌣′/ ⌣⌣/

We shall consider the second half-verse. From the standpoint of the location of pyrrhic feet, it is fully analogous to iambic trimeter: The same four variants in lines are possible as in iambic trimeter:

> (1) ⌣′/ ⌣′/ ⌣′/      (3) ⌣′/ ⌣⌣/ ⌣′/
> (2) ⌣⌣/ ⌣′/ ⌣′/      (4) ⌣⌣/ ⌣⌣/ ⌣′/

---

[29] The example for iambic trimeter was selected for simplicity. It was noted above that the formula $y = 0.28(x - 1)$, for iambic trimeter, does not agree very well with experimental data. More precise data for iambic trimeter will be given below.

TABLE 2

The Distribution of Stresses in Iambic Caesural Pentameter
(according to B. V. Tomashevsky)

| | 1 | 2 | 3 | 4 |
|---|---|---|---|---|
| | Rhythmic scheme of each half-verse type | Frequency of this type | Theoretical probability of the line | Experimental frequency of the line |
| **1st half-verse** | *Vskrichal Odul'f* <br> ∪ ′/ ∪ ′/ <br> *Iz glubiny* <br> ∪ ∪/∪ ′/ <br> *Krasavitsa* <br> ∪ ′/∪ ∪/ | $p_1$ 0.57 <br><br> $p_2$ 0.15 <br><br> $p_3$ 0.28 | $p_1q_1$ 0.206 <br> $p_2q_1$ 0.054 <br> $p_3q_1$ 0.101 <br> $p_1q_2$ 0.026 <br> $p_1q_3$ 0.338 | 0.208 <br> 0.057 <br> 0.097 <br> 0.028 <br> 0.335 |
| **2nd half-verse** | *Skazal mudrets bradatyj* <br> ∪ ′/ ∪ ′/ ∪ ′/∪ <br> *Pervonachal'ny nravy* <br> ∪ ∪/∪ ′/ ∪ ′/∪ <br> *Volshebnoyu krasoj* <br> ∪ ′/ ∪∪/ ∪ ′/ <br> *Bez predugotovlen'ya* <br> ∪ ∪/∪∪/∪ ′/ ∪ | $q_1$ 0.361 <br><br> $q_2$ 0.045 <br><br> $q_3$ 0.591 <br><br> $q_4$ 0.001 | $p_2q_2$ 0.006 <br> $p_2q_3$ 0.083 <br> $p_3q_2$ 0.013 <br> $p_3q_3$ 0.166 <br> $p_1q_4$ 0.006 <br> $p_2q_4$ 0.001 <br> $p_3q_4$ 0.003 | 0.007 <br> 0.086 <br> 0.010 <br> 0.173 <br> 0.003 <br> 0.003 <br> 0.003 |
| | | | Total types 12 | |

Combining the three forms of the first half-verse with the four types of the second yields twelve theoretically possible kinds of lines for iambic caesural pentameter. Here, the choice of the first half-verse in no way influences the choice of a second. Therefore, according to the rules of probability theory, the frequency of each of the twelve theoretically possible types of lines must be equal to the product of the frequencies predicted for those half-verses, of which a certain type of line is composed. If the frequency of a certain kind of line is not the product of the predicted frequencies of its component half-verses, this means that they are not independent and that the choice of the first is somehow connected with the choice of the second.

Tomashevsky's experiment (see Table 2) testifies to the independence of the various kinds of half-verses. In column 1, the rhythmic schemes of the half-verse types are listed. Column 2 shows the experimental frequencies of the types of first half-verse (designated *p* with the appropriate indices) and of the second half-verse (*q*, with appropriate indices). In column 3, theoretical probabilities are written for the combination of the first half-verse with the second (twelve in all), as calculated on the assumption that half-verse types are independent, i.e., by cross-multiplication of the probabilities for the corresponding kinds of half-verses; and in column 4 are written the experimental probabilities of the same combinations. A comparison of experimental with theoretical data does not contradict the hypothesis of independence. Essentially, this means that the second half-verse of iambic pentameter is constructed as an independent verse—an iambic trimeter—and its form is in no way connected with the form of the first half-verse.

Thus, in studying the distribution of pyrrhic feet in iambic caesural pentameter, it is sufficient to study the distribution of pyrrhic feet in the first half-verse, while for the second half-verse, one can use the data for iambic trimeter. Tomashevsky's application of the rule for calculating the probability of simultaneous occurrence of independent events made it possible to simplify the work considerably. The formula (see p. 110) and statistical data on the distribution of pyrrhic feet in various iambs make it possible to calculate mean values for the number and location of stresses for any iambic meter. Having obtained such data for Pushkin and other poets, we can construct comparable tables from which one can judge the individual peculiarities of the iambic meter of various poets.[30]

Since the distribution of metric variants even within an iamb with a certain number of feet is twice as individualized for the great poets, such tables can be used also for heuristics.

We have discussed only a few examples of the application of

---

[30] Here we take into account, of course, not only the distribution of pyrrhic feet but also the distribution of caesuras and several other characteristics. The tables mentioned are presented in B. V. Tomashevsky's study, "The Iambic Pentameter of Pushkin," in *Pushkin: sovremennye problemy istoriko-literaturnogo izucheniya* [*Pushkin: Contemporary Problems in Historical-Literary Study*], Kul'turno-prosvetitel'noe trudovoe tovarishchestvo "Obrazovanie," Leningrad, 1925.

statistical methods to the description of individual language facts. It seems to be generally true for the studies we have considered that by treating certain language phenomena as *random* (in the technical sense) and by studying them with statistical methods, the authors have discovered several regularities that could not have been found by another approach.

Choice of examples was dictated by the necessity of avoiding the use of the complex mathematical apparatus of probability theory in explaining them. Those desirous of becoming more familiar with the application of statistical methods in studying various language phenomena may refer to the following in addition to studies referred to above: L. R. Zinder [4], S. Saporta and D. Olson [36], J. B. Carroll [16], C. E. Shannon [37]. See also [20], [32] (phonetics, phonology, the statistics of letters and groups of letters); the works of P. Guiraud ( [24], [25] ); N. R. French, C. W. Carter, Jr., and W. Koenig, Jr. [21]; V. Garcia Hoz [22]; H. A. Simon [38]; V. H. Yngve [46]; and others—[23], [27], [28] (lexicology, syntax, questions of style). Also interesting are the articles of C. B. Williams [45] and G. U. Yule [47] on the length of the predicate in the works of various authors. Interesting materials are contained in a collection of articles on speech statistics [4], in the *Theses* of the First All-Union Conference on Machine Translation [7] and in those of the Conference on Mathematical Linguistics [8], and also in the bulletin *Mashinnyj perevod i prikladnaya lingvistika* [*Machine Translation and Applied Linguistics*].

For an introduction to probability theory and mathematical statistics, we would recommend E. S. Venttsel's work [3] and the introduction to N. Arley and K. R. Buch's book [1]; also A. M. Yaglom and I. M. Yaglom's book, *Veroyatnost' i informatsiya* [*Probability and Information*] [14]. All linguists should read a study by the outstanding Russian mathematician A. A. Markov, "Ob odnom primenenii statisticheskogo metoda" ["An Application of Statistical Method"] [6], in which the necessity of evaluating reliability in linguistic research was first demonstrated.

# BIBLIOGRAPHY FOR CHAPTER V

1. Arley, N., and K. R. Buch, *Vvedenie v teoriyu veroyatnostej i matematicheskuyu statistiku* [*Introduction to the Theory of Probability and Statistics*, John Wiley & Sons, Inc., New York, 1950], Izd-vo inostr. lit., Moscow, 1958.
2. Belyj, A. (Boris Bugaev), *Simvolizm* [*Symbolism; Book of Articles*], Library "Musagette," Moscow, 1910.
3. Venttsel', E. S., *Teoriya veroyatnostej* [*Probability Theory*], Fizmatgiz, Moscow, 1958, 575 pp.
4. Zinder, L. R., "Voprosy statistiki rechi" ["Questions on the Statistics of Speech"], *Materialy po mashinnomu perevodu*, Vol. I, Leningrad State University Press, Leningrad, 1958.
5. Gnedenko, B. V., and A. Ia. Khinchin, *Elementarnoe vvedenie v teoriiu veroyatnostej* [*Elementary Introduction to the Theory of Probability*], Gostekhizdat, Moscow, 1957, 144 pp.
6. Markov, A. A., "Ob odnom primenenii statisticheskogo metoda" ["An Application of Statistical Method"], *Izvestiya Imperialisticheskoj akademii nauk*, Series 6, No. 4, 1916, pp. 239–242.
7. *Tezisy konferentsii po mashinnomu perevodu, 15–21 maya 1958 goda* [*Theses of the Conference on Machine Translation, Moscow, May 15–21, 1958*], MGPIIYa, Moscow, 1958.
8. *Tezisy soveshchaniya po matematicheskoj lingvistike, 15–21 aprelya 1959 goda* [*Theses of the Conference on Mathematical Linguistics, April 15–21, 1959*], MVO SSSR, Leningrad, 1959.
9. Tomashevsky, B. V., *O stikhe: Stat'i* [*Poetry: Articles*], "Priboj," Leningrad, 1929.
10. Frumkina, R. M., "Nekotorye voprosy metodiki sostavleniya chastotnykh slovarej" ["Some Procedural Problems in Compiling Frequency Dictionaries"], *Mashinnyj perevod i prikladnaya lingvistika* [*Machine Translation and Applied Linguistics*], No. 2(9), 1959, pp. 23–37. (Translated: JPRS 3599, U.S. Joint Publications Research Service, August, 1960, pp. 16–28.)
11. Fuchs, W., "Matematicheskaya teoriya slovoobrazovaniya," *Teoriya peredachi informatsii* ["A Mathematical Theory of Word Formation," *Information Theory*, Colin Cherry, ed., Academic Press, Inc., New York, 1956, pp. 154–170], Izd-vo inostr. lit., Moscow, 1957, pp. 221–247.
12. Chebanov, S. G., "O podchinenii rechevykh ukladov 'indoev-

ropejskoj' gruppy zakonu Puassona" ["Subjecting the Speech Usages of the 'Indo-European' Group to Poisson's Law"], *Doklady Akademii nauk SSSR*, Vol. 15, No. 2, 1947, pp. 103–106.

13. Chistyakov, V. F., and V. K. Kramarenko, *Opyt prilozheniya statisticheskogo metoda k yazykoznaniyu* [*An Experiment in Applying Statistical Methods to Linguistics*], 1st edition, Izdatel'stvo Kubanskogo pedagogicheskogo instituta, Krasnodar, U.S.S.R., 1929.

14. Yaglom, A. M., and I. M. Yaglom, *Veroyatnost' i informatsiya* [*Probability and Information*], 2nd edition, 1960; originally *Wahrscheinlichkeit und Information*, VEB Deutscher Verlag der Wissenschaften, Berlin, 1960.

15. Apostel, L., B. Mandelbrot, and A. Morf, *Logique, Langage, et théorie de l'information*, Paris, 1957.

16. Carroll, J. B., "The Assessment of Phoneme Cluster Frequencies," *Language*, Vol. 34, No. 2, Part 1, 1958, pp. 267–278.

17. Condon, E. U., "Statistics of Vocabulary," *Science*, Vol. 67, No. 1733, 1928, p. 300.

18. Davenport, W. B., Jr., "An Experimental Study of Speech-Wave Probability Distributions," *Journal of the Acoustical Society of America*, Vol. 24, No. 4, 1952, pp. 390–399.

19. Estoup, J. B., *Gammes Sténographiques*, 4th edition, Paris, 1916.

20. Fowler, W. "Herdan's Statistical Parameter and the Frequency of English Phonemes," *Studies Presented to Joshua Whatmough on His Sixtieth Birthday*, E. Pulgram, ed., Mouton & Co., 's-Gravenhage, Netherlands, 1957, pp. 47–52.

21. French, N. R., C. W. Carter, Jr., and W. Koenig, Jr., "Words and Sounds of Telephone Conversations," *Bell System Technical Journal*, Vol. 9, April, 1930, pp. 290–324.

22. Garcia Hoz, V., *Vocabulario usual, común y fundamental*, Madrid, 1953.

23. Gougenheim, G., "La statistique du vocabulaire et son application dans l'enseignement des langues," *Revue de l'enseignement supérieure*, No. 1, 1959, pp. 154–159.

24. Guiraud, P., *Langage et versification d'après l'oeuvre de Paul Valéry*, C. Klincksieck, Paris, 1953.

25. ———, *Les charactères statistiques du vocabulaire*, P.U.F., Paris, 1954.

26. Hanley, M. L., *Word Index to James Joyce's "Ulysses,"* University of Wisconsin Press, Madison, Wisconsin, 1937 and 1951.

27. Harwood, F. W., and A. M. Wright, "Statistical Study of English Word Formation," *Language,* Vol. 32, No. 2, Part 1, April-June, 1956, pp. 260–273.

28. Herdan, G., "The Hapax Legomen: A Real or Apparent Phenomenon," *Language and Speech,* Vol. 2, Part 1, 1959, pp. 26–36.

29. Josselson, H. H., *The Russian Word Count and Frequency Analysis of Grammatic Categories of Standard Literary Russian,* Wayne State University Press, Detroit, Michigan, 1953.

30. Kaeding, F. W., *Häufigkeitswörterbuch der Deutschen Sprache,* Steiglitz bei Berlin, 1898; The Macmillan Co., New York, 1928.

31. Kuraszkiewicz, W., "Statystyczne badanie slownictwa polskikh tekstow XVI wieku," *Z polskikh studiów slawistycznych* (Prace jezykoznawcse i etnogenetyczne na 4. Medyznarodowy Kongress Slawistow w Moskwie, 1958), Wydawn. Naukowe, Warsaw, 1958, pp. 240–257.

32. Manczak, W., "Fréquence d'emploi des occlusives labiales, dentales, et vélaires," *Bulletin de la Société Linguistique de Paris,* Vol. 54, Fasc. 1, 1959, pp. 208–214.

33. Mandelbrot, B., "Structure formelle des textes et communication," *Word,* Vol. 10, No. 1, 1954, pp. 10–27.

34. Reed, D. W., "A Statistical Approach to Quantitative Linguistic Analysis," *Word,* Vol. 5, No. 3, 1949, pp. 235–247.

35. Saporta, S., "Frequency of Consonant Clusters," *Language,* Vol. 31, 1955, pp. 25–30.

36. ———, and D. Olson, "Classification of Intervocalic Clusters," *Language,* Vol. 34, No. 2, Part 1, 1958, pp. 261–266.

37. Shannon, C. E., "Prediction and Entropy of Printed English," *Bell System Technical Journal,* Vol. 30, January, 1951, pp. 50–64.

38. Simon, H. A., "On a Class of Skew Distribution Functions," *Biometrika,* Vol. 42, Part 3–4, 1955, pp. 425–440.

39. *Studies in Language Behavior: Psychological Monographs,* Vol. 56, No. 2, 1944.

40. Thorndike, E. L., and I. Lorge, *The Teacher's Word Book of 30,000 Words,* Teachers College, Bureau of Publications, Columbia University, New York, 1944.

41. Vander Beke, G. E., *French Word Book* (publication of the American and Canadian Committees on Modern Languages, Vol. 15), The Macmillan Co., New York, 1929.

42. Vey, M. A., "A propos de la statistique du vocabulaire tchèque:

examen des principales relations numeriques," *Slavia Occidentalis*, Vol. 27, No. 3, 1958, pp. 396–409.

43. Wagner, R. L., and P. Guiraud, "La méthode statistique en lexicologie," *Revue de l'enseignement supérieure*, No. 1, 1959, pp. 154–159.

44. West, M., *A General Service List of English Words with Semantic Frequencies and a Supplementary Word List*, Longmans, Green & Co., Inc., New York, 1953.

45. Williams, C. B., "A Note on the Statistical Analysis of Sentence-Length as a Criterion of Literary Style," *Biometrika*, Vol. 31, Part 3–4, February, 1940, pp. 356–361.

46. Yngve, V. H., "Gap Analysis and Syntax," *IRE Transactions on Information Theory*, Vol. IT–1–2, No. 3, 1956, pp. 106–112.

47. Yule, G. U., "On Sentence-Length as a Statistical Characteristic of Style in Prose: With Application to Two Cases of Disputed Authorship," *Biometrika*, Vol. 30, Part 3–4, January, 1939, p. 363.

48. ———, *The Statistical Study of Literary Vocabulary*, London, 1944.

49. Zipf, G. K., *Human Behavior and the Principle of Least Effort*, Addison-Wesley Publishing Company, Inc., Cambridge, Massachusetts, 1949.

# CHAPTER VI

# Information Theory and the Study of Language

## 1. General Remarks

For a scientific description of language as a means of communication, of language in its essential, communicative function, language must be compared with other systems used for the transmission of information. The problem was long ago presented in this manner by De Saussure, who asserted that language must be studied within the framework of a science of symbolic systems—"general semeiology" (see bibliography to Chapters I and II, [9], p. 30). The study of this aspect of language can now be put on an exact mathematical basis, thanks in part to the methods of information theory.

The need for studying language by the methods of information theory is based on practical necessity. Language is one of the most important means of transmitting information in human society, and only through the use of information theory can one obtain the data about language that are needed for working out effective means of transmitting language information by telegraph, telephone, radio, etc. ([3], [4], [11]).

The first attempts to study language by the methods of information theory led to inflated accounts of the wide perspectives that this theory opens to linguistics (see, for example, [26]). Further research has led to a more sober evaluation of the actual possibilities ( [29], [19] ). Information theory forces one to consider language as a code, and permits several properties of this code to be studied, using statistical models. One can form judgments regarding the fruitfulness of statistical models of language based on the concepts of information theory, these judgments being governed by the degree to which the models can be applied in solving "linguistic problems proper," i.e., problems that have been brought to light in the course of the past development of linguistics. But one must not forget that practical application of linguistics presents new problems of undoubted importance.

Before speaking of the linguistic applications of information theory, we consider it necessary to present several of its concepts that are especially essential for linguistics (see also the most popular existing presentations of information theory—[5], [10], [11] ).

## 2. The Concept of "Quantity of Information"

Information theory is an outgrowth of mathematics rather closely related to statistics. The foundations for information theory were laid in 1948 by the American scientist C. E. Shannon [37]. The theory has developed rapidly and successfully in the last few years. Information theory deals with the processes of transmission of information through communications systems. Related to communications systems are not only such technical apparatus as the telephone, the telegraph, and radio, but also language communication, the mechanism of reaction by an animal to an external stimulus, systems for traffic control, etc. We can represent any communication system schematically as in Figure 7.

Whatever is transmitted over a communication system is called a *message*. A communication system consists of a *source* initiating the message, a *transmitter* transforming the message into signals that can be transmitted along the communication channel, a *receiver* recreating the message from a sequence of signals, and a *recipient*. In any communications system, *noise* usually acts on the signal. By noise we mean any kind of random error arising unavoidably during the transmission of a signal. This is the idealized scheme. All of its parts are present in one form or another in any act of communication.

The purpose of a communication system is to transmit *information*. The concept of information is primitive, undefined. The decisive notion in the creation of the theory was the concept "quantity of information," because this provided a means for establishing a quantitative comparison of the "essential" properties of characteristically heterogeneous messages.

The concept of "information" is usually associated with an idea about some substantial communication of important news to the receiver-recipient. But information theory does not treat

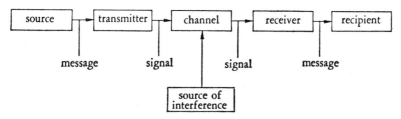

FIGURE 7. Schematic Representation of a Communication System.

the quantity of information in a message as a function of its substance or its importance. For this reason, information theory proposes an approach to communication, and to the information contained in it, that seems unnatural at first glance. It will be easier to understand the point of view of this theory if we note that information theory, including all its present applications, was at first closely bound up with the practical needs of engineers who were developing communication systems. From the communication engineer's point of view, the most essential attributes of a message are the time needed to transmit it, the complexity of the apparatus transmitting the signal, etc. Whether the message itself communicates a brilliant scientific discovery or asserts that $2 \times 2 = 4$, whether it warns of an emergency in a factory or forecasts the weather—the problem consists of transmitting the message in the most rapid and accurate manner to the recipient-receiver. The content of a message, its reliability, importance, etc., are not essential. The only property of a message that, from this point of view, *is* essential is its *statistical structure*. We shall explain this further.

If we abstract the content and qualitative facets of a message, then all messages resemble one another; they all represent some sequence or other of symbols.[1] Such, for example, are language messages, telegraphed messages in Morse code, etc. The symbols composing a message form a finite set—the alphabet.

In any meaningful message, various symbols are encountered with various frequencies, so that the relative frequency of appearance of symbols in various sections of homogeneous messages is more or less constant. This permits one to consider the occurrence frequency of a symbol in a message to be a definite characteristic of this symbol, or an inherent property of it. This characteristic is called a *probability*[2] (the probability of appearance of a symbol $i$ is designated $p(i)$).

Another important property of the message is that various groups of symbols also occur in it with different frequencies; thus, for example, if the message is a written text in Russian, the group of letters $t'$ will occur quite frequently, while the combination $o'$ is practically excluded. This means that in addition to its probability, symbol $i$ possesses a *conditional probability*,[3] i.e., the probability of its occurrence in a message under the condition that the preceding symbol be some $j$ (designated $p_j(i)$). The probabilities and conditional probabilities of symbols determine the statistical structure of the message.[4]

If the message interests us only from the standpoint of its sta-

---

[1] Regarding messages that seem to have another nature, see p. 132.

[2] For the sake of simplicity, one can say that a symbol's probability is its relative frequency in a rather lengthy message (actually, such a representation of probability is a very rough one; in the bibliography for Chapter V, see [5], a popularized version of probability theory). For example, let a message consist of a dot-dash sequence. A section of it 1,000 symbols long is studied. In this sample, the dot occurs 750 times, and the dash occurs 250 times. Then one can say that the probability of the dot is 0.75 and that of the dash is 0.25. Thus, the probability is always expressed by a proper fraction. We note that the sum of the probabilities of all symbols that can occur on a single trial is always equal to unity. If the probabilities of all symbols are the same, then that for each symbol equals $1/n$, where $n$ is the total number of symbols.

[3] Regarding the concept of "conditional probability," see [5]. Conditional probability can be calculated from the simple probability of individual symbols and the probability of combination of symbols by the following formula: $p_j(i) = p(j, i)/p(j)$, where $p(j, i)$ is the combinatorial probability of the symbols $(j, i)$.

[4] Compare the concept of the "statistical structure of text" on p. 97, which has a slightly different meaning.

tistical structure, then the process of creating a message can be represented as follows. Let us assume that a series of *trials* is being made. The outcome of each trial consists of the appearance of one of the symbols of the alphabet, so that the occurrence frequency of various symbols in repeated trials is determined by the probability of the symbols. The sequence of symbols appearing during this process is the message. The model described represents the creation of a message (i.e., communication) as a *probabilistic process*. Thus, the mechanism for creating a message is analogous, for example, to an imaginary mechanism that casts dice and writes down the results of each cast (i.e., the numbers from 1 to 6), combining them into infinite sequences. Although we use a probabilistic model to describe the process of message production, we can hardly suppose that real messages are formed in just this way. The model does not pretend to describe the real process. It is important only that the statistical structure of real messages be exactly the same as it would be if they were created by the mechanism described.

The reason that a knowledge of the statistical structure of messages is so important for their transmission over communications systems will become fully clear only from further discussion (see Sec. 4.2); for now, we shall confine our discussion to just a short preliminary explanation. If one is transmitting a message in which certain words or phrases are repeated particularly often, then it is desirable to tell the receiver-recipient of these messages to write the words down in some abbreviated form. However, such abbreviation is possible only if one knows just how frequently the different words and phrases occur.

If the probability of occurrence of a symbol at a certain point in the message does not depend on what symbol or symbols preceded it, then one can say that the symbols in a message are *independent*. An example of a message that consists of independent symbols might be the "communication" created by casting dice. Among messages consisting of *dependent* symbols, some may be initiated by a particular type of probabilistic process, namely, a *Markov process* (or Markov chain). In such a message, the probability that a certain symbol $i$ will occur depends on the nature of the immediately preceding symbol $j$, and not on that of any part of the message preceding $j$. If the dependency between symbols extends further, to a longer chain preceding the present symbol, then one speaks of a *complex Markov process;* in any Markov process, however, the number of symbols influencing the probability of occurrence of a particular symbol must be finite.

Information theory develops the means for quantitatively comparing different messages from the standpoint of the indicated statistical properties. For this purpose, the concept of a "quantity of information in the communicative symbol" is also introduced. At first, we shall deal only with messages consisting of sequences of independent symbols. Let us consider the process whereby an addressee receives a message. Since we are assuming a situation wherein more or less similar messages are transmitted frequently, it is natural to believe that, even before the next symbol in the message is transmitted, the receiver knows the set of possible symbols (the alphabet) and the probability of each symbol. If the total number of symbols in the alphabet is small (e.g., two), and their probabilities are quite different (e.g., if one symbol's probability is 0.99 and that of the other is 0.01), then the situation before reception of the symbol contains almost no indeterminacy for the recipient; he can predict in advance and with a high degree of accuracy which of the symbols will be transmitted. The indeterminacy of the situation increases as the number of symbols in the alphabet increases. Where the number of symbols is fixed, it is greatest if their frequencies are equal. Thus, the degree of indeterminacy before reception of a symbol depends on the number of possible symbols and on their probabilities. As Shannon has shown, it is useful to assume that the degree of the indeterminacy is connected with the probability of the symbols by the following equation:

$$H_1 = - [p(1) \log_2 p(1) + p(2) \log_2 p(2) + \cdots + p(n) \log_2 p(n)],$$

where $H_1$ is the degree, or value, of indeterminacy, $n$ is the number of symbols in the alphabet, and $p(1)$, $p(2)$, . . . , $p(n)$ are the probabilities of symbols from the 1st to the $n$th. Once a symbol has been received, the indeterminacy is completely eliminated. Therefore, it is natural to think that the degree of indeterminacy characterizing a situation before reception of the next symbol is a measure of the quantity of information in the symbol received. Consequently, one can call the value of $H_1$ a quantity of information, which can be measured by the formula cited above. If we call the probability of a symbol $p(i)$, where $i$ takes the values 1, 2, . . ., $n$, then this expression can be written in an abbreviated form, using the summation sign ($\Sigma$):

$$H_1 = - \sum_{i=1}^{n} p(i) \log_2 p(i). \tag{1}$$

In the special case where all symbols are equally probable (as in the case of dice), formula (1) has a simpler form:

$$H_1 = \log_2 n. \tag{2}$$

To see this, let the number of symbols in the alphabet be $n$; then the frequency of each is $1/n$, and formula (1) will contain $n$ equal components; hence,

$$H_1 = - n \frac{1}{n} \log_2 \frac{1}{n} = - \log_2 \frac{1}{n} = - (\log_2 1 - \log_2 n) = \log_2 n.$$

When one speaks of the quantity of information in a symbol from a message, he does not mean the information in the concrete symbol (e.g., in the letter $a$ of a message written in the letters of the Russian alphabet). From the standpoint of information theory, such a question as: "What information is contained in the letter $a$?" is meaningless. Only the information in the *average* symbol is being measured, i.e., the average quantity of information in one symbol as it is frequently iterated in the message; in fact, since the amount of information is being compared with the value of indeterminacy, this amount really characterizes the situation before reception of the symbol, rather than the symbol itself.[5]

---

[5] Generally speaking, from formula (1), one can derive an expression for the amount of information in a particular concrete symbol $a_1$:

$$H^{a_1} = - \log_2 p(a_1) = \log_2 \frac{1}{p(a_1)}$$

(hence, the widespread expression "message containing little information" = "a message possessing high probability"). However, the value $H^{a_1}$ can hardly have any substantial application.

To be able to measure the value of the information, one must have not only a method of measuring (as defined by formulas (1) and (2)), but also a *unit of measurement*. The latter is selected arbitrarily (analogously to the way in which, for example, a unit for measuring length, weight, or other physical magnitudes is selected). The unit of quantity of information is the information derived from a symbol in a message if the alphabet consists of two symbols having equal probability; this unit is called a binary unit (abbreviated *b.u.*, or simply *u*).

The value defined by formula (1) possesses several important properties:

(1) The value of $H_1$ is always positive (the probability is expressed in fractions, and the logarithm of a fraction is a negative number; but a minus sign is used before the parenthesis).

(2) If the alphabet consists of only one symbol, then $H_1 = 0$. (If there can only be one result for any trial, then its probability is 1; thus, we obtain $H_1 = (1)(\log_2 1) = 0$.)

(3) For a fixed number of symbols, $H_1$ is maximal when the probabilities of all symbols are equal. This property can be illustrated by the following example. Let the alphabet consist of four characters. If the probabilities of all four are equal (i.e., if the probability of each symbol is 0.25), then according to formula (2):

$$H_1 = \log_2 4 = 2\,u.$$

If the probabilities are not equal, the quantity of information for the same number of symbols will be less. Thus, for the distribution of probabilities 1/2, 1/4, 1/8, and 1/8, the quantity of information per symbol equals:[6]

$$H_1 = -\,[(1/2)(-1) + (1/4)(-2) + (1/8)(-3) + (1/8)(-3)]$$
$$= 1/2 + 1/2 + 3/8 + 3/8 = 1.75\,u.$$

(4) If the message consists of a sequence of independent symbols, the amount of information in a pair of adjacent symbols is equal to the sum of the values expressing the amount of information in each symbol. Let the number of symbols in the alphabet equal $N$. Let us assume, for the sake of simplicity,

---

[6] For simplicity in calculation, one can use a table of $p(i) \log_2 p(i)$; see [11], pp. 305–308.

that the symbols have equal probabilities, so that the quantity of information in each symbol will be $\log_2 N$. Since the symbols are independent, the number of possible different pairs is $N \cdot N$ (each of the $N$ symbols in the first place may be combined with any of the $N$ symbols in the second place). If we consider a pair of symbols as one symbol, then according to formula (2), the amount of information in the pair is $\log_2 N \cdot N$; but $\log_2 N \cdot N = \log_2 N + \log_2 N$. Thus, the values characterizing the quantity of information in independent symbols can be expanded to obtain at the same time the value of the information contained in the combination of symbols. This property of the measure of information is called the property of *additivity*. If we measured the information not by the logarithm of the number of symbols but, for example, by the number of symbols, then the information in a pair of independent symbols would equal not the sum but the product of the information in each.

Suppose one had to determine the amount of information in not just one symbol but in a combination of $m$ symbols. The property of additivity allows us to define the quantity of information $H^m$ in a combination of $m$ symbols under the condition of independence of the symbols by the following simple formula:

$$H^m = mH_1. \tag{3}$$

The four properties enumerated above would seem to agree with our intuitive ideas about the measurement of information: It seems natural that the number defining the amount of information should be positive, that the quantity of information in a communication consisting of repetition of the same single symbol should be zero,[7] that the information in independent symbols can be totaled. In our presentation, we first introduced

---

[7] The following selection from L. Carroll's *Alice in Wonderland* is a curious example of this position. Alice got lonesome and had no one to talk to but her cat. But how is one supposed to hold a conversation with a cat? ". . . If they would only purr for 'yes,' and mew for 'no,' or any rule of that sort, . . . so that one could keep up a conversation! But how *can* you talk with a person if they always say the same thing?" Information theory would evaluate the quantity of information in a cat's message exactly as Alice did.

[The quote the author gives is incorrectly attributed to *"Alice in Wonderland"*; it appears in chapter 12 of *Through the Looking-Glass and What Alice Found There.*—Tr.]

a definition of the quantity of information and then showed how our intuitive ideas concerning the measurement of information were reflected by it. Obviously, however, the agreement is strictly superficial; the properties enumerated corresponded to demands that could be imposed on the measurement of information, as reflected in formula (1). Thus, the requirement corresponding to property (1)—the positive character—necessitates the minus sign; the requirement emerging from property (4)—the possibility of combining information—causes us to introduce logarithmic measurement,[8] etc.

One of the most important properties of the expression proposed by Shannon as a definition of the concept of a "quantity of information" consists of its being very similar to the expression used to define an important concept in thermodynamics— the concept of "entropy." The difference between these expressions lies only in the fact that in the expression for entropy the minus sign is not present, i.e., entropy always has a negative value. This similarity in the expressions is not accidental; rather, it reflects the internal identity of these concepts. In physics, entropy is usually described as a measure of the random character of the structure of a physical system (for example, gas contained in a sealed vessel). Another very important approach to understanding physical entropy has become possible (see [40], p. 95, notes, and [1], pp. 16–18 and 200–212): No physical system is fully defined; while we can determine such properties of the system as its temperature and pressure, we cannot define the exact location and velocity of all the molecules composing the system, even though these very phenomena are what, in the final analysis, cause both the temperature and the pressure. Entropy can be thought of as a measure of insufficient information, i.e., a measure of the inexactness of our knowledge concerning the position and velocity of individual molecules, after all possible measurements have been made.

Because of the similarity of the expressions, the value $H_1$ is often called *entropy* (although it would be more exact to speak of "negative entropy").[9] We shall use the words "quantity, or amount, of information" and "entropy" as synonyms.

---

[8] The fact that the logarithm is taken with base 2 is connected with the choice of the unit of quantity of information.

[9] [$H_1$ is infrequently called negentropy in English.—Tr.]

## 3. The Amount of Information in a Sequence of Dependent Symbols

Up to now, we have considered only the special case of messages consisting of sequences of independent symbols. However, messages in which symbols are dependent are much more frequently encountered. An example of such a message is a sequence of letters in a text, or a sequence of dots, dashes, and spaces, as in Morse code, etc.

Let us first take the case of a message in which statistical dependencies exist only between two adjacent symbols (i.e., a message involving only a simple Markov process). Let $a_1$, $a_2$, $\ldots$, $a_n$ be the symbols of the alphabet; we choose any particular symbol, which we relabel $a_1$. The indeterminacy characterizing the situation before the occurrence of the next symbol can be calculated using formula (1), except that in place of the probabilities $p(i)$, we must insert conditional probabilities for the symbols, to wit: the probabilities of the symbols when the preceding symbol was $a_1$, namely, $p_{a_1}(i)$. The value $H_{a_1}$ (the amount of information in a symbol for the fixed condition $a_1$) is then calculated as follows:

$$H_{a_1} = - \sum_{i=1}^{n} p_{a_1}(i) \cdot \log_2 p_{a_1}(i). \qquad (4)$$

Clearly, the value $H_{a_1}$ for the same message will vary with different selections of $a_1$. Thus, if we take a written text in English as our sample of a message and consider the symbol $a_1$ to be the letter $q$, then the value $H_{a_1}$ will be nearly zero, since the situation "after $q$" is hardly indeterminate at all; one can predict with assurance that the following letter will be $u$ ($q$ is almost always followed by a $u$). Elsewhere, the degree of indeterminacy is considerably higher. The *average* indeterminacy arising for all situations in which one symbol in the message is already known is called *conditional information*, or *conditional entropy*, and is calculated using the following formula:

$$H_2 = p(a_1) \cdot H_{a_1} + p(a_2) \cdot H_{a_2} + \cdots + p(a_n) \cdot H_{a_n}, \qquad (5)$$

where $H_2$ is the conditional entropy, $H_{a_1}$, $H_{a_2}$, $\ldots$, $H_{a_n}$ are entropies for fixed conditions, while $p(a_1)$, $p(a_2)$, $\ldots$, $p(a_n)$ are the probabilities of the symbols $a_1$, $a_2$, $\ldots$, $a_n$, respectively.

In information theory, the basic characteristic of a message is usually considered to be only the value $H_2$; however, in linguistic applications the value $H_{a_1}$ is also used, as we shall see in Sec. 7.4.

Sometimes it is simpler to calculate the value of the conditional entropy in another fashion; if one knows the probabilities $p(j, i)$ for all pairs of symbols in the message, then one can calculate the value of $H^2$—the quantity of information in a pair of symbols—using formula (1):

$$H^2 = - \sum_{i=1}^{n} \sum_{j=1}^{n} p(j, i) \log_2 p(j, i).$$

Afterwards, the value of $H_2$ can be defined:

$$H_2 = H^2 - H_1, \tag{6}$$

where $H_1$ is the amount of information in the same message, as calculated from formula (1). It follows from formula (6) that the conditional entropy is equal to the difference between the information in a pair of symbols (the values of $H^2$) and the information in one symbol, as calculated on the assumption that the symbols are independent (the value of $H_1$).

One can calculate the conditional entropy in messages analogously, where statistical dependencies are distributed not just among two symbols but over three or more. For a sequence of symbols, where statistical dependencies exist only between two adjacent symbols, the fundamental characteristic is the value of $H_2$—conditional entropy of the first order; if dependencies exist among as many as three symbols, then one must define the value of $H_3$—conditional entropy of the second order—for complete characterization of the sequence; in messages where dependency extends over $m$ symbols, a value $H_m$, i.e., a conditional entropy of the $(m - 1)$th order, must be defined.

Let dependency be distributed among $m$ symbols. We shall designate a certain $i$th combination of $m$ letters by $B_i$; then, the probability of the combination $B_i$ will be designated $p(B_i)$. The amount of information $H_m$ in a combination of $m$ dependent symbols is equal to

$$H^m = - \sum_{i=1}^{n} p(B_i) \cdot \log_2 p(B_i),$$

where $n$ is the number of different combinations of $m$ symbols.

The conditional entropy $H_m$ of the $(m-1)$th order equals the difference between the quantity of information in the combination of $m$ symbols and that in a combination of $m-1$ symbols, i.e.,

$$H_m = H^m - H^{m-1}. \tag{7}$$

In general, a message in which the statistical bonds extend over a great distance can be characterized by the value $H_0$ (the amount of information if all symbols are equally probable), by the value $H_1$ (the amount of information if all symbols are independent), by the value $H_2$ (the amount of information if dependency extends only to two adjacent symbols), by $H_3$, etc. The values $H_0$, $H_1$, $H_2$, etc., represent *sequential approximations* to the value $H$—the real amount of information per symbol.

Thus, the amount of information increases with an increase in the number of different symbols in the message, whereas it decreases, for a given number of symbols, with the presence of statistical limitations in the message (i.e., with inequality of probabilities and presence of dependencies among symbols). Sometimes it is necessary to compare different messages from the standpoint of the magnitude of the statistical limitations. For this purpose, the concepts of relative entropy $H_{\text{rel}}$ and of *redundancy R* (see [38]) are introduced. These values are calculated as follows:

$$H_{\text{rel}} = \frac{H}{H_{\text{max}}}, \tag{8}$$

where $H$ is the real quantity of information in a symbol, and $H_{\text{max}}$ is the maximal possible amount for a given number of symbols ($H_{\text{max}} = H_0 = \log_2 n$, where $n$ is the number of symbols in the alphabet). Redundancy is a value directly connected with the relative entropy:

$$R = 1 - H_{\text{rel}}. \tag{9}$$

Relative entropy and redundancy are expressed in per cents. If all the symbols in a message are equally probable and independent, redundancy equals zero; the greater the statistical limitations, the higher the redundancy.[10]

---

[10] Additional explication of the concept of "redundancy" can be given after questions regarding encoding have been considered; see Sec. 4.2.

## 4. Some Transformations of Messages

### 4.1 QUANTIZATION

Whenever we describe the process of transmission of information, we proceed from the assumption that a message is *discrete*, i.e., that it is a sequence of individual symbols selected from a finite alphabet. In addition, there exist messages seemingly possessing a basically different nature. Take the telephone, for example. The functional principle of telephone apparatus lies in the fact that sound waves are transformable into electric signals that can be transmitted over wires. The amplitude of the sound wave can vary continuously; it takes on a countless number of different values, since the values of the amplitude during consecutive moments of time can differ very little from each other. But a continuous message cannot, in practice, be transmitted in an unchanging form; in the first place, it is impossible to transmit every momentary value of the amplitude of a sound wave—they can be transmitted only at definite intervals; in the second place, it is impossible to achieve an absolutely exact measurement of the value of the amplitude, and the value is noticeably coarsened during transmission. The operations performed in all instances of transmission of continuous messages bear the name of *quantization*.

Quantization occurs not only in technical communications systems; analogous processes occur during transfer of information by human beings (see Sec. 5.3).

The essence of quantization can be represented more precisely by the following example: If one takes a discrete scale such that an initially continuous change in some value is broken up into a series of discrete values, one can then transmit, in selected intervals of time, not the actual magnitude of the value, but rather that which corresponds to the nearest level specified on the scale. Thus, the value is "approximated" with a specified degree of accuracy, and transmission of the communication is once again reduced to the transmission of numerical values chosen from a finite alphabet.

## 4.2 Coding

The transmission of messages over great distances often demands a change in their form; e.g., a telegram, originally written as a sequence of letters, is transformed into a sequence of dots and dashes and then into a sequence of electric impulses. Such transformations are called *encoding*. There are various types of codes. A code is characterized as an alphabet of elementary symbols with rules for their combination. A set of symbols in one code directly related to a symbol or combination of symbols in another code is called a code combination. There are codes in which all the combinations are the same length. Such codes are called regular (Morse code is not regular; the average length of the combination of symbols for *e* (" .") is one, while that for *o* is three: "— — —"). Aside from the length of a code combination, one main characteristic of a code is the total number of symbols in the alphabet. Quite frequently a code is used the alphabet of which consists of only two symbols. Such codes are called binary.

One can take advantage of the statistical structure of a message and use codification to transmit the latter in the shortest possible time. Let us consider the following example (from Shannon [37]; treated in greater detail in [5] and [8] ).

Suppose we have a message in an alphabet consisting of four letters with the probabilities $1/2$, $1/4$, $1/8$, and $1/8$, respectively. If one encodes this message with a regular binary code in which each code combination is two symbols long, then a section of the message containing 1,000 letters will consist of 2,000 code symbols. One can also encode this message with another code, an irregular one, giving the first letter the combination 0, the second 10, the third 110, and the fourth 111.[11] If, in a communication 1,000 letters in length, the first letter occurs about 500 times, the second 250, and the third and fourth 125 times each, then the total length of the message when encoded in the sec-

---

[11] Since our code is irregular, and there is no special combination for spaces, the construction of code combinations must satisfy the following requirement: No combination can be the beginning of another, or else it will be impossible in decoding to separate unambiguously the parts of a message that correspond to code combinations. For this reason, one cannot use the combinations 1, 11, 01, etc., in this code.

ond way will be about 1,750 symbols $(500 \cdot 1 + 250 \cdot 2 + 125 \cdot 3$
$\cdot 2)$, i.e., 250 symbols less than if it were encoded in the first
way. Consequently, the second code makes it possible to transmit a message in less time.

Thus arises the problem of optimal codes, i.e., codes that
would guarantee the possibility of transmitting a message with
a given quantity of information using the shortest possible sequence of symbols. The basic principles for constructing optimal codes are reducible to the following. If a message consists
of independent symbols not having equal probabilities, then
the optimal code must assign to the most frequent symbol the
shortest code combination, and conversely: The least frequent
must be assigned the longest combination (as in our example).
If the symbols in a message are not independent, then it would
be wise to substitute code combinations, not for individual symbols, but for groups of symbols in the output message (since, ow-
ing to the dependency between symbols, various groups will be
encountered with varying frequencies, and some might not even
occur at all).

An important result of information theory is that it permits
one to determine how far he can go in shortening a message
through the use of intelligent encoding. One of Shannon's the-
orems says that the limit to which this reduction of the length
of a message can be carried with binary encoding is defined by
the quantity of information in the message. Thus, in our example, the amount of information per symbol is

$$H_1 = - \ (1/2 \log_2 1/2 + 1/4 \log_2 1/4 + 1/8 \log_2 1/8 + 1/8 \log_2 1/8)$$
$$= 1.75 \ u.$$

In a message 1,000 letters long, the quantity of information is
1,750 $u$, and the second code for this message is optimal.[12]

Coding is used not only for greater efficiency but also to improve the transmission of information. For the latter purpose,
self-correcting codes are employed. The principle on which
these codes are constructed is that not all possible combinations
of symbols are used as code combinations, but only a part (i.e.,

---

[12] We can now make the concept of redundancy more concrete. The redundancy in a message amounts to 50 per cent if, in translating it from a certain
code into the optimal code with the same number of symbols, we find that its
length has decreased by 50 per cent.

code combinations are constructed according to specific rules). A distortion of one of the symbols changes a code combination into a set of symbols that is not a legitimate code combination. If the distinction among combinations is great enough, one can not only find out that an error has occurred but also predict rather accurately which actual combination should take the place of the distorted one. The construction of combinations according to specific rules signifies a conscious introduction of redundancy into the code.

The very immediate connection between the quantity of information in a message and an economical encoding of it is a proof of the thesis formulated in the beginning of this chapter, namely, that the statistical structure of a message, when evaluated with the aid of the concepts of information theory, is the only property of communication that can be considered essential from the standpoint of transmitting it over communications systems.

The value of the concept of information developed by Shannon is not limited to its broad possibilities for application in communications technology. It proves fruitful in many other areas as well. Let us cite several examples. The concept of information is very important in the study of several processes of human transmission and reception of information. In one particular experiment [32], the degree of accuracy in understanding words under extremely noisy conditions was measured. Difficulty in recognizing words (and the information in a word) was found to depend on knowledge of the number of words from which a particular word was chosen.[13] If the hearer knows, for example, that the word to be spoken is one of ten figures (from zero to nine), then the word will be understood correctly even under extremely noisy conditions. But if he does not know this, he will not comprehend the word even 50 per cent of the time. In this way, difficulty in comprehension depends on the amount of information contained in the word.

The broad applicability of Shannon's concept of information is also illustrated in experiments on the rate of performance of several processes connected with the transmission of information in the human organism [10]. The experiment is as fol-

---

[13] [Other pertinent factors being held constant.—Tr.]

lows. The subject must react in response to $n$ different conditions; e.g., in response to $n$ different signals he must push one of $n$ knobs. It turns out that the time needed to complete such a reaction increases as a logarithmic function of the number of signals. This phenomenon can be explained only if we accept the idea that "messages" in the human nervous system are optimally encoded, and therefore the length of a message (and, consequently, the time needed to transmit it) is proportional to the amount of information contained in it.

We shall now consider ways of applying the concepts introduced above to linguistic research.

## 5. Language as a Code with Probabilistic Limitations

The study of language using the methods of information theory requires the construction of a definite model for language. The model gives a simplified picture of language because it reflects only certain of its properties, ignoring the others. The extraction of certain properties with the use of the model has great significance, since this permits the study of certain properties by exact methods.

The model on which we shall base our discussion is that of language defined as *a code with probabilistic limitations*. Two aspects must be elucidated: (1) In what respects can language be said to approximate a code? (2) Why do the probabilistic limitations in language deserve the attention of linguists?

### 5.1 LANGUAGE AND CODE

On pp. 133 *ff.* we discussed various types of codes; there we were referring to artificial, specially developed notations for messages which, until they are encoded in a particular manner, exist in another, "natural" form—e.g., as a sequence of words or letters. However, the word "code" can be understood in another, broader sense—as any method of writing a message. According to G. A. Miller ( [30], p. 7), "any system of symbols that, by prior agreement between the source and destination, is used to represent and convey information will be called a code." In this broad sense, language, too, can be called a code.

The identification of language with code is based primarily on the fact that, in language as in technical codes, description of the combinability of elements plays an important role. For a technical code, the rule for combination of symbols is the main characteristic. In language, aside from the combinatory capabilities of the units, many other properties are essential; but the importance of describing language from the standpoint of the combinatory capabilities of its units cannot be doubted. The limited nature of this capability is one factor defining the structure of language: The combinability of phonemes is no less important a characteristic of a phonological system than the composition of the phonemes and their grouping from the standpoint of phonological oppositions; description of word formation and word alternation is the determination of the laws of combinability of morphemes within a word; analysis of the syntactic structure of language absolutely demands a description of the combinatory capabilities of syntactic word classes within a phrase or clause. A description of combinability can be constructed analogously for meaningless units such as the phoneme or syllable, and for meaningful ones, i.e., for words, morphemes, etc. From the standpoint of the combinatory capabilities of language units, we shall equate the description of language with the description of code.[14]

The identification of language with code sometimes occurs for another reason. In fact, for all technical codes except repetitions of code combinations, an indication of the coding rules is necessary. These rules define a method of comparing a combination in a particular code with a symbol or group of symbols in another code. Usually, a message undergoes several transformations on the way from the source to the receiver, i.e., translations from one code to another. The code applied in the part of the communications system nearest to the source can be called *primary*, relative to that used further on, i.e., the *sec-*

---

[14] The importance of describing the codelike aspects of language (in our sense) was first emphasized in the distributional theory of language (see the expansion of this theory developed by Z. S. Harris in his *Methods in Structural Linguistics*, The University of Chicago Press, Chicago, Illinois, 1951). His theory, however, proceeds from the assumption that description of the codelike properties of language is restricted at present by the limited possibilities of exact description of language, which is absolutely untrue.

*ondary* code (for the distinction between primary and secondary codes, see [2] ). The interrelation of language with codes,
that serve as primary codes with respect to language, is still a
very complicated and unclear problem. Therefore, in speaking
of the codelike properties of language, we shall imply not the
monovalence of the coding rules but only the existence of definite laws for the combinatory characteristics of the units.

## 5.2. DETERMINATION OF A CODE BY ANALYSIS OF MESSAGES

In technical codes, the man designing the code determines
the rules for combining units. In language, the rules are not
immediately given. There exists only the totality of messages
encoded in this code (text), and the properties of the code
must be determined by analysis of messages. However, determination of the rules of a code from messages is complicated
by real difficulties. We shall discuss some of the more basic of
these in detail.

The rules governing the combinability of units of a message
differ qualitatively. For example, let us represent messages as
sequences of words. In real texts, limitations, especially those
due to the language's grammar, are imposed on the combinatory capacities of words; the presence of such limitations causes,
for example, a near-zero probability of finding the following
sequence of words in any (grammatical) Russian utterance: *iz
trudami matematicheskij po lingvistika.*[15] Not only grammatical
but also semantic limitations are imposed on real text. As a result of the existence of such limitations, one would hardly encounter in real text such a statement as, for example, the following: *Kvadrat vypil vsyu trapetsiyu* [The square drank up
the entire trapezoid]. Grammatical limitations are inherently
different from restrictions on meanings. If it seems natural to
consider grammatical limitations on text as caused by the code
(i.e., as codelike), then, obviously, restrictions on meaning have
no relation to the code but, rather, are characteristics of the
communication itself. In fact, all real messages originate from
some concrete situation or other. The sentence about the square

---

[15] [No interpretation of this sequence could make it satisfy Russian rules of
grammatical agreement, word order, etc.; it is "ungrammatical."—Tr.]

has not been encountered because the corresponding situation has not occurred; but if it had occurred, such a sentence would have been created, and it would not have contradicted the norms of the Russian language, unlike the utterance before it, which was introduced as an illustration of the breaking of code rules. Consequently, semantic limitations of the text are naturally considered to be noncodal. (Regarding this, see [20]. )

The formulation of laws for the combinability of language units in the form of determinate rules demands that essentially linguistic, codelike restrictions be separated from those characterizing the message itself and having no relation to the code. However, the criteria that would permit the separation of the different types of restrictions are not clearly enough defined. Thus, the probability is very high that in all Russian texts created up to now we shall not find such combinations as: *vchera pojdu* [I shall go yesterday] (although *skoro pojdu* [I shall go presently] does exist), *inogda ubezhal* [He had sometimes run away][16] (compare *bystro ubezhal* [He ran away fast]), *derevyannoe ispol'zovanie* [wooden use] (compare *polnoe ispol'zovanie* [complete use]), etc. Is the absence of such combinations in text caused by the code of language or by "meaning"? Obviously, different descriptions will provide different answers to this question.

The second class of complicated problems is related to the following circumstance. Language communications can be studied on several "levels"[17]—on those of phonemes, syllables, morphemes, words, letters, etc.; the combination of units on one level is affected by limitations reflecting laws of combinability of units not only on that level, but on others as well. Thus, the phoneme combination [szh] is unallowable by the phonological code of Russian; the combination [zhasas] is permissible by that code but is not found in messages, because it does not correspond to any meaningful unit of the language; the combination [sazh—ám] is not allowed for by morphological laws, i.e., by the laws governing the combinability of phonemes in words,

---

[16] [The verbal aspect indicates a unique action, as *"He had sometimes run away once."*—Tr.]

[17] By "level," we mean the "aspect" or "standpoint" from which we consider a language communication. A level is characterized by the type of discrete units of which we consider a communication to be composed.

while the combination [k sázhu] is excluded by the laws of syntax. In this way, phoneme chains are restricted, as are all other levels of languages.

If we make it our problem to describe the laws governing combinability in the form of structural, qualitative, determinate rules, then we must separate the limitations affecting the laws of one level from all others. But the criteria of separation, as in the preceding instance, can hardly be formulated clearly enough.

Finally, one more type of difficulty lies in the fact that messages can break the laws of a particular code. We have stated above that the word combination *iz trudami matematicheskij po lingvistika* has an extremely low probability of being encountered in real messages, but it is not excluded entirely. Actually, such "utterances" can occur in real messages, since they can be made by someone not too familiar with the code of a particular language. Such distorted phrases occur not infrequently in artistic literature, as, for example, the Chinese girl Sin Bin's remark in Vs. Ivanov's tale, *Bronepoezd 14–69:* "*Moya Kitaya v poryadok nado?*" ["Mine of China in order must?"], or "*Tvoya moya ne ponimaj!*" ["Thine mine do not understand!"].

We can cite yet another example of broken code rules in communications—an example relating to the area of phonology. In Russian, the combination of [n] with a consonant at the beginning of a word is not ordinarily possible (compare the removal of this combination in such abbreviations as *NSO, NTO,* etc., which are pronounced with an initial [e]; then compare *SNO, MKhAT,* etc., pronounced without the [e], since unallowable combinations of consonants at the beginning of a word are not present in these cases). However, the combination of [n] with a consonant is possible in "exotic" words (e.g., *nganasane, nkundo*).

## 5.3. STATISTICAL APPROACH TO THE COMBINATORY PROPERTIES OF LANGUAGE UNITS

Because of the complexity, multiplicity, and close overlapping of the various laws that determine the structure of a language text, the laws of language code cannot be described in the same way as the rules for technical codes (e.g., as a simple iteration of combinations, like Morse code, or as an indicator of certain restrictions, like self-correcting codes). Since laws based on a qualitative analysis of the combinatorial capacities of units on a certain level are always limited and incomplete, it is useful, in addition, to formulate laws for combinability in the form of statistical laws. In this case, the probabilistic process may be the text-producing model; in particular, one can consider a Markov process to be such a model (either simple or complex). If we are to construct a model for text in the form of a simple Markov process, we must define the probabilities of all symbols for this text, as well as the conditional probabilities of the first order. For example, if one represents Russian text as a sequence of vowels and consonants—phonemes—then a Markov model for this text can be given as in Table 1, where $C$ stands for consonant, $V$ for vowel.[18] The probabilities of the corresponding transitions are shown in the table.

TABLE 1

$$p(C) = 0.58; \qquad p(V) = 0.42$$

| $p_j(i)$ | | $i$ | |
|---|---|---|---|
| | | $C$ | $V$ |
| $j$ | $C$ | 0.26 | 0.74 |
| | $V$ | 0.99 | 0.01 |

The simple Markov process still gives a poor approximation of real text, since the statistical bonds in language text act at great distances; thus, the probability of encountering a certain word at the end of some article or even a thick book depends, in essence, on the kind of words composing its title [8]. There-

---

[18] For data on conditional probabilities of Russian vowels and consonants, see L. R. Zinder, "O lingvisticheskoj veroyatnosti" ["On Linguistic Probability"], *Voprosy yazykoznaniya*, No. 2, 1958, pp. 121–125. (Translated: JPRS 6445, U.S. Joint Publications Research Service, Series "K": *Soviet Developments in Information Processing and Machine Translation*, December, 1960, pp. 7–14.)

fore, if we construct a statistical model of a given text to calculate the dependency of one symbol only on the preceding one, then, of course, this model will not reflect the long-range connections. However, for the same text one can construct a sequence of statistical models that will reflect the statistical regularities of the text much more accurately (i.e., reflect the dependencies throughout a large section of text), since the chains of symbols created by the model will in every case "resemble" the text more closely. We shall cite several examples of the "product" of statistical models for Russian and English (taken from [11] and [40] ).

*I. Examples for Russian (The message is studied at the letter level.)*

1. A zero-order approximation ("text" consists of the same alphabetic symbols as real text, but the statistical regularities of real text are not reflected at all; the symbols are randomly distributed):

*sukherrob'dsh yaykhvshchikhjtoifvna rfenvshtdfrpkhshchgpch'-kizryas.*

2. An approximation of the first order (the letters occur with real-text frequencies):

*syntsyya' oerv odng 'uemklojk zbya entvsha.*

3. An approximation of the second order (the simple Markov process; combinations of two letters occur with real-text frequencies, i.e., conditional probabilities of the first order are taken into account):

*umarono kach vsvannyj rosya nykh kovkrov nedare.*

4. An approximation of the third order (each three-letter combination occurs with the same frequency as in ordinary text):

*pokak pot postivlennyj durnoskaka nakonenno zne stvolovil se tvoj obnil'.*

5. An approximation of the fourth order (four-letter combinations occur with the frequencies found in ordinary text):

*vesel vrat'sya ne sukhom i nepo i korko.*

*II. Examples for English (The message is considered on the word level.)*

1. An approximation of the first order (the words occur with real-text frequency):

*representing and speedily is an good art or come can different natural here he the a in come the to of to expert gray.*

2. An approximation of the second order (two-word combinations occur with real-text frequency in English):

*the head and in the frontal attack on an English writer that the character of this point is therefore another method for the letters that the time of who ever told the problem for an unexpected.*

The statistical approach proposed for describing combinatory capabilities possesses several internal restrictions. In such an approach, the combinability of language units cannot be described individually and in detail. The statistical approach does not allow for a reflection of the qualitative diversity of relations among elements (e.g., the multiplicity of the grammatical relations among words), or for the separation of qualitatively distinct regularities. The "syntactic rules" of language in such a model provide only for the conditional probability that one element will follow another. However, the formulation of laws for a language code, in the form of statistical rules of the indicated sort, possesses a certain basic worth: The statistical laws of combinability can be made explicit from immediate observation of text; in order to formulate such rules, one does not have to develop criteria for the idealization of a text that absolutely must be introduced in order to divide limitations among various levels and to separate code restrictions from noncode ones.

Thus, a premise for the study of language, using the methods of information theory, is to approach language as a code and to formulate laws for this code in the form of statistical rules of a definite type. This is exactly what we have in mind when we say that language study through the methods of information theory is based on a model of language as a code with probabilistic restrictions.

## 5.4. The Discrete and Continuous Quality of a Speech Signal

Our model for language is based on the assumption that speech is a sequence of discrete units. Linguistics also proceeds from this assumption; one of its main problems is the construction of alphabets of discrete language units. But this, especially for spoken utterances, is complicated by basic difficulties. The carrier of a spoken message is a sound wave; described acoustically, from the standpoint of oscillatory frequency, time, and intensity, it is continuous. This continuity yields to discreteness only when a man receives the signals; a quantization of the signal occurs, transforming the signal into a sequence of discrete units. Such a discrete unit, for the phonetic aspect of language, is usually called a phoneme. However, the principles according to which speakers induce this quantization still remain unexplained; at any rate, this process cannot be "produced" by a machine.

The latest achievements in the technique of sound analysis (particularly the invention of the spectrograph) have given birth to a number of attempts to separate out the acoustical invariant for a large class of physically distinct sounds accepted by speakers as one phoneme. If such an invariant had been found, we would have arrived at the point at which a "rounding" of the acoustical characteristics of sound must occur during its reception. However, these attempts have failed.

The work of R. O. Jakobson, R. M. Fano, and M. Halle[19] has been most valuable for explanation of the principles of quantization, for they have shown that acoustical correlates can be defined not for phonemes, but for the *distinctive features* of phonemes. A distinctive feature is not an absolute, but a relative, characteristic of sound; it is a constancy of *distinction* between a certain sound and other sounds pronounced by the speaker in analogous circumstances. Thus, the "rounding" is evidently oriented toward the distinctive feature rather than toward the phoneme.

[19] See R. O. Jakobson, R. M. Fano, and M. Halle, *Preliminaries to Speech Analysis*, Technical Report No. 13, Massachusetts Institute of Technology, Cambridge, Massachusetts, 1952.

Moreover, it has been shown that all features can be considered as binary, i.e., as taking two values. For example, the feature of "consonant versus vowel" has the values "vowel" and "consonant," and that of "voicedness" has the values "voiced" and "unvoiced," etc.; thus, the process of transmission and reception of spoken messages is a process of encoding and decoding the message in a binary code. The authors introduce a list of twenty features on which the phonological distinctions made in most of the world's languages are based (each language "selects" as its distinctive features a particular group from among these twenty).

However, the number of unsolved problems in this area is very large, and there exists no reliable and generally acceptable list of phonemes and distinctive features for any language.

Linguistics asserts that language communication can be regarded as a sequence of discrete units of another kind: meaningful units—morphemes or words. However, the construction of an alphabet of semantic units connected with the analysis of meaning is an even more difficult problem than that of composing an alphabet of units for the phonetic aspect of language (see Chapter II).

A message written in a natural language has a clearly expressed discrete character. The alphabet of letters for a written message is known to every literate person, and the entire word list can be formulated, at least for limited application of the language, on the basis of appropriate texts (if one always considers the bounds of a word to be spaces and different words to be different sequences of letters between spaces, then this procedure does not present any basic difficulties).

Most of the more accurately conducted experiments on language using information theory have been carried out by individuals generally unfamiliar with data (admittedly inconclusive) about the alphabets of discrete units of language "proper" [i.e., spoken language—Tr.] that linguists have presented. For this reason, one cannot be surprised that most research deserving of attention relates to "written language."

Contemporary linguistics does not recognize written language as a fully justified object of research, since it considers written language a secondary (and, consequently, artificial) phenomenon. However accurate this attitude may be, written language cannot be disregarded.

In contemporary society, written speech—the bearer of information to be transmitted to the public—plays an enormous role, and the practical value of research in this area is indisputable. Data on written language are therefore definitely worthy of attention for their own sake. Furthermore, the entire methodology and general principles of linguistic research, using the concepts of information theory, do not change in any essential respect when applied to spoken language as well; it is important only that one know how to write a spoken message as a sequence of discrete units. Thus, the fact that most published data refer to written language must not lead to the conclusion that the value of the results is restricted.

## 5.5. STATISTICAL DATA ON LANGUAGE

As we have said, a statistical model of language is proposed as a model for the probabilities and conditional probabilities for all the symbols of the alphabet. The relative frequencies of phonemes and letters are constant, at least for a limited area of linguistic usage (i.e., for texts in a specific area of science, for the speech of a certain language community, etc.). Hence, one can speak of the probabilities of these symbols for a given, restricted "language," or even for language as a whole. No complicated procedure is needed to obtain reliable data on the probabilities of combinations of two or three letters or sounds (for statistical data on phonemes and letters in Russian and English, see [18], [21], [36] and the bibliography for Chapter V, [4] and [49]; for data on the frequencies of Russian phonemes, see the table on p. 150).

The frequencies of words vary greatly from one text to another. This is especially true of rare words, because in the existing frequency dictionaries (see bibliography for Chapter V, [22], [29], [30], and [40]), one can only consider the conclusions for the first thousand most frequent words (see bibliography for Chapter V, [10]) to be reliable. There exist practically no data on the frequencies of phrases.

Moreover, the connections among words possess such a strong "distant action" (see p. 141) that any Markov model based, for example, on conditional probabilities of the second order yields a very poor approximation to the sense-sequences of words in real text (for examples, see above).

Thus, we possess syntactic data that are sufficient only for constructing statistical models of language at the levels of letters and phonemes. We do not consider current conclusions about probabilities or the composition of an alphabet to be sufficient for constructing statistical models of language at the level of meaning units.

## 6. Measurement of Information and Redundancy in Natural Languages

### 6.1. CALCULATION OF THE AMOUNT OF INFORMATION IN LETTERS AND PHONEMES ON THE BASIS OF THEIR PROBABILITIES

In order to calculate the amount of information per unit of language code, using formulas (1)–(9) (see Secs. 2 and 3), one must know the probabilities and conditional probabilities of these units. Quantity of information and conditional entropy have been calculated for several European languages on the basis of available statistical data ([4], [15], [18], [38]).[20] The results are presented in Table 2. For written utterances, the quantity of information per letter is shown;[21] for spoken, per phoneme. Data for speech are only present for Russian; the dashes in the table indicate the absence of data.

We shall consider the process of calculating the quantity of

---

[20] Many of the numerical data cited below are not conclusive and need further verification. Even in such cases, however, the methodology whereby they were obtained is independently interesting, and they therefore deserve our attention.

[21] In calculating from the Russian written material, it was agreed that the total number of letters is 32: *e* and *ë*, ь and ъ are considered to be the same letter; space is counted as a letter. In English, the space is also considered a letter; the counts for German, French, and Spanish are based on an alphabet of 26 letters (space is not counted as a letter, and the above-the-line symbols— i.e., accents and umlauts—are not counted); the difference between the value of $H_0$ for English and those for other European languages is partially explained by this difference in conventions: ($\log_2 27 = 4.76$; $\log_2 26 = 4.70$).

TABLE 2

| Amount of informa-tion (conditional entropy) | | $H_0$ | $H_1$ | $H_2$ | $H_3$ |
|---|---|---|---|---|---|
| Language | Form | | | | |
| Russian | spoken | 5.38 | 4.76 | 3.69 | 0.70 |
| | written | 5.00 | 4.35 | 3.52 | 3.01 |
| English | written | 4.76 | 4.03 | 3.32 | 3.10 |
| German | written | 4.70 | 4.10 | — | — |
| French | written | 4.70 | 3.98 | — | — |
| Spanish | written | 4.70 | 4.01 | — | — |

information in spoken Russian in further detail (these calculations are described in a paper by C. Cherry, M. Halle, and R. O.
Jakobson [18]). The amount of information is calculated on
the basis of a representation of speech as a string of phonemes.
Generally speaking, the string of phonemes does not reflect all
the information contained in the utterance. Aside from certain
"sense-distinguishing" information, the usual province of linguistics, the utterance also contains an enormous amount of additional information: It transmits emotional overtones, has a
logical impact, gives information about the speaker (one can
recognize the speaker by his voice), etc. The amount of "sense-
distinguishing" information in a portion of speech corresponding to the phoneme does not exceed 7 $u$ [i.e., 7 bits—Tr.] (the
number of phonemes in a language is in no instance greater
than $2^7$: Certain Caucasian languages contain the most phonemes, but even there the number does not exceed 80).[22] In

---

[22] The function of distinction is fulfilled not only by phonemes but also by
such "nonsegmental" elements as stress and intonation; the authors consider
stress to be one of the differential attributes of phonemes, but they ignore the
sense-distinguishing role of intonation.

modern communication lines, speech is usually transmitted within a frequency band of 7,000 cps; this means that for an average transmission rate of 10 phonemes per second, the quantity of information in a piece of speech corresponding to a phoneme amounts to 5,600 $u$.[23] Hence, it is evident what a small part of all the information in speech sound is "sense-distinguishing" and is preserved when speech is represented as a string of phonemes (for several measurements of the value of "nonsense-distinguishing" information, see [10], p. 109).

The authors start with the fact that there are 42 phonemes in Russian (see Table 3). The value $H_1$ for Russian text was calculated from data on phoneme frequency. Selections of conversation were used for the frequency count, as described and transcribed by A. M. Peshkovsky[24] (the text contained 10,000 phonemes in all). If the frequency is known, then the amount of information can be calculated from formula (1) as follows:

$$H_1 = - \sum_{i=1}^{n} p(i) \log_2 p(i)$$

$$= - (0.13 \log_2 0.13 + 0.10 \log_2 0.10 + \cdots + 0.0007 \log_2 0.0007)$$

$$= 4.76 \, u.$$

(The terms on the right are $p(i) \log_2 p(i)$ for all phonemes; see Table 3.)

The values $H_2$ and $H_3$ are calculated from data on the frequencies of two- and three-phoneme combinations. Frequencies were calculated on the same text; only phoneme combinations existing within a word were considered (boundaries within complex words and compounds were treated as word boundaries). On the basis of the frequencies of two-phoneme combinations, it is possible to calculate the amount of information in a combination using formula (1):

$$H^2 = - \sum_{i=1}^{n} \sum_{j=1}^{n} p(j, i) \log_2 p(j, i) = 8.45 \, u;$$

hence, from formula (6) (p. 130), $H_2 = H^2 - H_1 = 3.69 \, u$. The

[23] See R. M. Fano, "Information Theory Point of View in Speech Communication," *Journal of the Acoustical Society of America,* Vol. 22, 1950, p. 691.

[24] See A. M. Peshkovsky, *Desyat' tysyach zvukov* [*Ten Thousand Sounds*] (a collection of articles), Gosizdat, Leningrad-Moscow, 1925, pp. 167–191.

TABLE 3

Phoneme Frequency and Distinctive Features[a]

| Phoneme | Phoneme frequency ($p(i)$) | $\log_2 p(i)$ | $p(i) \cdot \log_2 p(i)$ | No. of distinctive features |
|---|---|---|---|---|
| а | 0.1316 | 2.94 | 0.387 | 4 |
| п | 0.0977 | 3.85 | 0.328 | 6 |
| т | 0.0602 | 4.05 | 0.244 | 9 |
| 'а | 0.0539 | 4.23 | 0.228 | 4 |
| j | 0.0457 | 4.45 | 0.202 | 2 |
| н | 0.0392 | 4.66 | 0.183 | 6 |
| 'о | 0.0379 | 4.72 | 0.179 | 5 |
| с | 0.0359 | 4.80 | 0.172 | 8 |
| 'е | 0.0343 | 4.86 | 0.167 | 5 |
| к | 0.0284 | 5.14 | 0.146 | 7 |
| в | 0.0273 | 5.15 | 0.140 | 8 |
| 'л | 0.0243 | 5.38 | 0.131 | 6 |
| у | 0.0240 | 5.40 | 0.129 | 6 |
| л | 0.0232 | 5.42 | 0.126 | 8 |
| р | 0.0230 | 5.45 | 0.125 | 4 |
| н' | 0.0221 | 5.50 | 0.121 | 6 |
| л | 0.0212 | 5.55 | 0.118 | 4 |
| ш | 0.0207 | 5.56 | 0.115 | 6 |
| м | 0.0202 | 5.64 | 0.114 | 6 |
| ц | 0.0197 | 5.65 | 0.111 | 5 |
| т' | 0.0196 | 5.65 | 0.111 | 9 |
| д | 0.0177 | 5.81 | 0.100 | 9 |
| д' | 0.0162 | 5.95 | 0.096 | 4 |
| 'у | 0.0153 | 5.96 | 0.091 | 6 |
| р' | 0.0133 | 6.20 | 0.083 | 4 |
| з | 0.0130 | 6.25 | 0.081 | 8 |
| л' | 0.0126 | 6.30 | 0.080 | 9 |
| б | 0.0119 | 6.39 | 0.075 | 8 |
| х | 0.0102 | 6.60 | 0.067 | 5 |
| г | 0.0091 | 6.80 | 0.062 | 7 |
| в' | 0.0089 | 6.84 | 0.061 | 8 |
| ж | 0.0089 | 6.84 | 0.061 | 6 |
| ф | 0.0085 | 6.86 | 0.058 | 8 |
| с' | 0.0085 | 6.86 | 0.058 | 8 |
| щ | 0.0059 | 7.40 | 0.044 | 9 |
| м' | 0.0056 | 7.50 | 0.043 | 6 |
| б' | 0.0052 | 7.60 | 0.039 | 8 |
| п' | 0.0050 | 7.64 | 0.038 | 8 |
| к' | 0.0036 | 8.10 | 0.029 | 7 |
| з' | 0.0021 | 8.90 | 0.018 | 8 |
| ф' | 0.0008 | 10.30 | 0.008 | 8 |
| г' | 0.0007 | 10.50 | 0.007 | 7 |

[a] From Cherry, Halle, and Jakobson [18].

value $H_3 = 0.7$, obtained by Cherry *et al.*, is clearly too low. As a matter of fact, not all combinations were considered during the calculation (see [18], p. 36). In addition, the text length—10,000 phonemes—is obviously insufficient for accurate estimation of the frequencies of three-phoneme combinations.

The technique for obtaining data on the quantity of information in a letter of written text does not require further explanation.

However, the values $H_1$, $H_2$, and $H_3$ do not yield a very close approximation to the actual information per text symbol, since they account only for the statistical dependencies within two to three symbols, whereas the span of these dependencies is, in fact, much broader. One cannot obtain more accurate data on the quantity of information in language text by the same means, since calculation of the frequencies of combination for strings of more than three letters or phonemes is excessively unwieldy and cannot be performed practically by hand.

C. E. Shannon [38] proposed an indirect method of calculating the amount of information per letter. First, one must calculate the value $H_1$ for a word. This value can be calculated from word frequencies. Shannon used G. Dewey's frequency dictionary [21]. (In this dictionary, all different strings of letters between two spaces are considered different words, since all the forms of a word are considered different words, while homographs are the same word.) The amount of information in an English word is 11.82 $u$. The average length of a word in English is $s = 4.5$ letters (see bibliography for Chapter V, [49] ); a space lengthens a word by one letter. If the quantity of information per combination of 5.5 letters of text averages out as 11.82 $u$, then the information per letter is 11.82 $u/5.5 = 2.14$ $u$. This calculation permits calculation of the statistical bonds over spans of five letters of text and thus yields a closer approximation to the actual amount of information per letter of text. (In general, identification of the amount of information per word with the amount per average combination of $s + 1$ letters is not entirely proper; since statistical bonds among the letters within a word are, on the average, stronger than those existing among five arbitrary letters, the amount of information per combination of $s + 1$ letters will be greater than the amount per word—see [10].)

Analogous calculations were performed for French, German, and Spanish [15]. For these languages, there exist no dictionaries showing individual form frequencies; frequency is given for each word as a whole—all forms—for which reason the identification of the quantity of information per word with the average quantity for $s + 1$ letters of text is even less acceptable. The results of calculating the amount of information per letter by this means are presented in Table 4. (The data for English are presented for the sake of comparison, as calculated from a similar dictionary.)

TABLE 4

| English | French | German | Spanish |
|---------|--------|--------|---------|
| 1.65 | 3.02 | 1.08 | 1.97 |

### 6.2. Experimental Methods for Determining the Amount of Information and Redundancy

An approximation of a higher order to the quantity of information per letter can be obtained by several experimental methods developed by Shannon [38]. The main difficulty in calculating the amount of information in language text, as is evident from what has been said, lies in the fact that one must take into account statistical dependencies that are active over rather long spans. It is possible, however, to discover the statistical structure of a text by means other than the calculation of combination frequencies. Every man who speaks a particular language possesses a knowledge of the statistical structure of text in that language, albeit unconsciously. This knowledge manifests itself especially in the fact that when someone is asked to guess the following—call it the $n$th—letter in a text in which the $n - 1$ preceding letters are known to him, his guesses will not be entirely haphazard; they will be based on an intuitive knowledge of the probabilities and conditional probabilities of letters.

After performing enough letter-guessing experiments, one can estimate the probability, for each given number of preceding letters, that a following (*n*th) letter will be guessed correctly at the first, second, etc., attempts (since there are 27 letters in the English alphabet—i.e., 26 letters plus the space—the maximum number of attempts is 27). Shannon has shown that there are sufficient data in guess probabilities to calculate the conditional entropy of the $(n - 1)$th order, i.e., the value $H_n$ (or rather, one can find the interval within which the entropy is to be found, i.e., the upper and lower bounds[25]).

In Figure 8, we present a graph constructed from Shannon's data to show the decrease in the quantity of information per

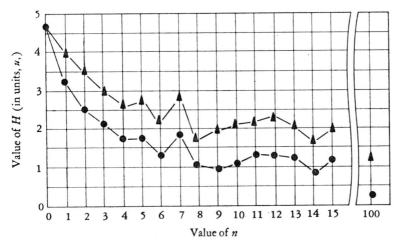

Value of *H* (in units, *u,*)

Value of *n*

FIGURE 8. Information, *H,* per Letter as a Function of the Number, *n,* of Letters.

letter as the number of letters increases, when the dependencies among letters are taken into account in calculating amount of information. (The value *H*—the amount of information—is rep-

---

[25] The upper and lower bounds of the quantity of information are defined by the following inequality:

$$\sum_{i=1}^{n} i(q_i^n - q_{i+1}^n) \log_2 (i) \leq H_n \leq - \sum_{i=1}^{n} q_i^n \log_2 q_i^n$$

where $q_i^n$ is the probability of guessing a letter at the *i*th attempt when the $(n - 1)$th letter is known. For further details, see [11].

resented as a function of $n$, where $n$ is the number of letters known to the subject as he makes his guesses.)

The redundancy of a given language can be calculated from data on quantity of information, with the same approximation (using formula (9), p. 131). Calculated from $H_3$, the redundancy of Russian is 39.8 per cent; that of English is 30.7 per cent. The approximate value of the redundancy can also be found by means of the following very simple experiment. Someone is made to guess letter after letter in a text of a definite length (e.g., a selection 100 letters long every time); if the next letter is not guessed correctly, the subject is told the right letter, and the experiment continues. We cite as an example the results of one experiment in English. On the upper line, the entire selection is given; on the lower line, only those letters that had not been guessed; the space between words is counted as one letter.

*The room was not very light a small oblong reading lamp on*
*\_\_\_\_roo_____not\_v\_\_\_\_li_____sm\_\_\_obl\_\_\_\_rea_____o\_*
*the desk shed glow on polished wood but less on the shabby*
*\_\_\_d_____glo\_\_o\_\_p\_ls_____o\_\_\_bu\_\_l\_s\_o_____sh\_\_\_\_*
*red carpet.*
*re\_\_c\_\_\_\_*

There are 129 letters in all in the selection; 89 letters—i.e., 69 per cent—are guessed correctly; hence redundancy is evaluated at 69 per cent. The figure obtained as a result of the experiment, when the latter is conducted on a large enough number of selections, can be accepted as an approximate value for the redundancy of a given language.

This method is particularly interesting because the experiment here can be conducted not only on letters, but on words as well. (In the previous guessing experiment, letters could not be exchanged for words: The maximum number of attempts for letters is limited by the length of the alphabet, whereas for words, the number of attempts can prove too great.)

Analogous experiments have been made in guessing a message represented as a string of phonemes. D. G. Fry [25] obtained a redundancy for English text of 55 per cent. However, these experiments apparently yield a lower per cent of redundancy just because "guessing games" are more unusual for phonemes. The end of the road for experimental research on the redundancy of spoken language is not as yet in sight.

6.3. The Upper Limit of Redundancy

From his experiments, Shannon obtained the value of information only for $n = 15$ and $n = 100$, whereas the increase in
redundancy over this interval is rather significant (see Figure
8). It is important to determine how far redundancy will increase as the amount of text selected increases. Is there a limit
beyond which an increase in the amount of text will not be accompanied by increase in redundancy (i.e., some maximum distance over which the statistical bonds among text symbols have
effect)? These questions were posed in a paper by N. G. Burton and J. C. R. Licklider [16].

Figure 9 shows the results of a determination of the redundancy $(R)$ for $n = 2, 4, 6, 8, 16, 32, 64, 128,$ and $10,000$. Re-

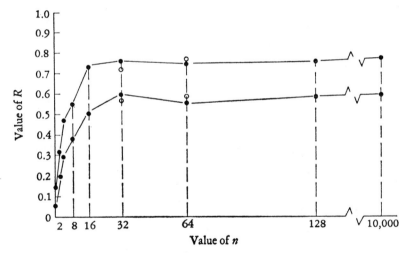

FIGURE 9. Redundancy, $R$, per Letter as a Function
of the Number, $n$, of Letters.

dundancy was estimated by Shannon's method (see pp. 152-154).
The two curves correspond to the upper and lower limits of
redundancy. As $n$ increases from 0 to 32, a sharp increase in the
redundancy is observed, but with further increase in the context from 32 to 10,000, no essential increase in redundancy takes

place. Thus, the increase in redundancy with increase in context is not infinite. The extreme redundancy for English lies in the interval between 55 and 75 per cent, while the span of activity of the statistical bonds among the letters in text is about 30 letters.[26]

### 6.4. A Statistical Model of Language on the Level of Meaning Units

Up to now, we have dealt with language only on the levels of phonemes or letters. Attempts to construct statistical models of language on the level of meaning units are most interesting [24]. As we have already said, construction of statistical models of language at this level is complicated by the difficulty of obtaining statistical data, or even an alphabet of units, on this level. These difficulties can be overcome, however, if a highly formalized language is studied; in this case, the "language" of pilots was analyzed, or rather the language used in a strictly confined situation: The notes used for the research were recordings of radio conversations between pilot and control tower during landing. (Notes were made during 100 landings.)

Not the word, the morpheme, or any of the elements usually dealt with by linguists were considered to be the elementary (nonexpanded) symbols. The authors felt that a message was rather a sequence of "semantic messages," or "elements of information," i.e., more or less complete elementary utterances. A list of these elements was composed in this way. The landing process was divided into several parts or "situations"; for each such situation, a complete list of possible utterances was made, and then the utterances were split into semantic elements. In language expression, "semantic elements" are usually short statements having a highly specific structure from the standpoint of ordinary language; sometimes these are individual words. Thus, the utterance: *"Langley Tower, || aircraft 611, || two miles out, || landing instructions, please"* is split into four such elements (their bounds are defined by vertical lines).

---

[26] For $n = 32$ and $n = 64$, an iterative experiment was performed, as called for by the fact that the redundancy for $n = 64$ was lower than the redundancy for $n = 32$.

The authors do not formulate criteria by which to be guided when splitting the elementary semantic units; they consider it sufficient to indicate that such criteria depend on the intuition of people familiar with this "language," and that this intuition, in most cases, led different people to identical results. We emphasize the fact that a list of "content elements" is being discussed, not the division of some language units or other; for this reason, such synonymous expressions as *gear down*,[27] *gear green, three green, gear down and locked with three green lights* (meaning "go more slowly") are considered to be the same unit.[28]

After a list of the semantic elements in all messages had been made, the redundancy caused by differences in frequency and by restrictions on combinability of elements was determined. The total redundancy is 80 per cent (the message is understood to be everything said by the pilot in the course of the entire landing); the redundancy caused by unequal probabilities is about 30 per cent, while that caused by dependencies among the elements is 50 per cent. In calculating redundancy, the authors took, for $H_{max}$, the information contained in one semantic element under the conditions of equal probability and independence of elements ($H_{max} = 9 \ u$); from the total number of messages that could have been transmitted at the observed rate, however, one reaches an even higher figure for redundancy. To determine over-all redundancy, one must change over to a count of the quantity of information in a section of phonemes or letters corresponding to one semantic element. From the authors' calculations, the redundancy is $R = 0.8$, whence we compute that the relative information $H_{rel} = 1 - R = 0.2 = 20$ per cent; actually, the value of the relative information has to be decreased by a factor of 4. If we assume that a 10-letter sequence corresponds, on the average, to a semantic element, then $9 \ u$ [9 bits—Tr.] per semantic element is equivalent to $1.1 \ u$ per letter. The maximum amount of information per letter attainable with 26 letters is $4.70 \ u$, i.e., about four times more. Con-

---

[27] [Here the original has *glar down*, apparently a misprint.—Tr.]

[28] Numerals presented a special problem in drawing up the list. In order not to complicate the number of semantic elements, numerical information is handled separately.

sequently, the final value for the relative information is about 5 per cent, whereas the total redundancy amounts to approximately 95 per cent (which corresponds with the data of other research on the same "language" [23], using a statistical analysis of utterances written as strings of letters).

The sharp increase in redundancy, as compared with the level generally characteristic for language, is, of course, related to the fact that a highly specialized language was subjected to analysis. Data on redundancy in specialized languages are very interesting to linguists, especially from the following standpoint: The main cause of redundancy in a language is, as we have explained, the fact that a message is produced in a narrowly restricted situation. A comparison of the redundancy in different specialized languages might well aid in an estimation, however approximate, of what fraction of text redundancy must be ascribed to the influence of the situation, i.e., to restrictions outside of the code.

## 7. Linguistic Interpretations of Information and Redundancy

Data on amount of information and redundancy are undoubtedly most valuable to communications technology; in human society, information is transmitted constantly and in great quantity. Most of this information is expressed via some one of the natural languages. Language code possesses a very high degree of redundancy; for this reason, the degree of economy that would be accomplished from the development of effective codes for natural languages is enormous. However, we shall not pursue the technical application of data on the quantity of information and redundancy in language (e.g., see [3] and [11]), but rather we shall take a look at several of the possibilities that information theory opens up for linguistics. These possibilities are not entirely obvious, and it is difficult to fit them into a coherent system. Therefore, we shall confine ourselves to indicating various methods and problems. In the majority of cases, final results are still not available, so that one can only speak of a more or less valid approach to the problem.

## 7.1. A COMPARISON OF LANGUAGES FROM THE STANDPOINT OF REDUNDANCY

The levels of redundancy of various languages apparently lie within certain narrow limits, permitting one to speak of a level of redundancy of 60 to 70 per cent as a universal property of language in general (of course, the present data are restricted to European languages). This fact is interesting for several reasons; in particular, one can place it in immediate relationship with another quantitative regularity: The data on a rather large number of languages suggest that in any language the average length of the minimum meaningful unit (the morpheme) is inversely proportional to the number of phonemes in the phonological system.[29] We can easily illustrate this relationship with the following "extreme" cases. In Hawaiian, whose phonological system contains only 13 phonemes in all, most morphemes consist of two syllables (i.e., 4 phonemes, on the average); moreover, very many morphemes consist of three or more syllables, while there are almost no one-syllable morphemes. On the other hand, in some Caucasian languages containing around 70 phonemes, almost every consecutive phoneme in a word forms an independent morpheme. For all the cases in between, about the same ratio obtains. The presence of such a relationship is natural, if one approaches language as a "rationally constructed code"; the morphemes in a language must be "encoded" with strings of phonemes. All morphemes could be distinguished from one another by means of a small number of phonemes—two would do; but, in this case, the length of the code combination for each morpheme would be very great. The more phonemes in a phonological system, the shorter the morphemes must be, or else coding would be too redundant. Thus, if a tendency really exists for redundancy to be constant in language, the relation indicated is a quite natural consequence of this tendency. Unfortunately, our conclusions regarding redundancy in various languages are still quite incomplete. In order to unify the different quantitative regularities of languages into

---

[29] See C. F. Hockett, *A Course in Modern Linguistics,* The Macmillan Co., New York, 1958, p. 93.

one system, it is very important that we investigate whether there exists any connection among redundancy, number of phonemes, and average word length in languages.

Of course, it is evident that one can speak of the relative nearness of the levels of redundancy in various languages only as a general tendency from which divergencies cannot fail to occur, while the differences among languages from the standpoint of redundancy are most interesting in themselves. A language's redundancy is the result of restrictions on the combinability of units and is, therefore, immediately connected with the presence in the language of a definite structure (in the sense discussed on p. 137). Thus, redundancy can be a quantitative measure of the "structuredness" of language and can form the basis for a typological comparison of different languages. It would be very interesting, for example, to compare the redundancies in languages, assigning different roles to morphology within the grammatic structure, especially in Russian and English. The present data (such as the fact that $H_3$ is 9 per cent greater for written Russian than for written English) force us to propose that the redundancy curve for Russian will increase significantly more rapidly than that for English.

A comparison of various languages in terms of their redundancies would give a more precise meaning to evaluations of the relative effectiveness of those languages, or of one language at different stages in its development, and would make the content of the concept of "progress in language" more exact. The idea of "progress in language" occupies a large place in O. Jespersen's works.[30] But, in practice, Jespersen identified progress in language with the tendency to "analytism," by which he meant a decrease in the use of morphology for the expression of syntactic bonds on account of word order. It would be interesting to explain how qualitative changes are connected, according to Jespersen, with change in the value of redundancy in a language, and whether there exist certain regularities for the change in redundancy during the development of different languages. An explication of such quantitative regularities would

---

[30] See O. Jespersen, *Efficiency in Linguistic Change*, E. Munksgaard, Copenhagen, 1941.

allow one to predict the direction of further development of a language, beginning with a quantitative analysis of its contemporary condition.

One could also ask about the coding effectiveness of various languages for the "exact same content" (see bibliography for Chapters I and II, [25]). If we believe that the content of a text remains the same when translated into another language, then the relationship between the quantities of information in texts, where one is the translation of the other, must indicate the "semantic weight" of one unit of information in the different languages. (The amount of information in a text, which is in no way connected with the content of that text, is determined from the number of symbols in the alphabet and by the statistical regularities of combinations in the corresponding languages, and naturally does not remain constant in translation.)

However, the following interesting fact was found upon comparison of the amounts of information in two texts that were identical in content—one in German and the other in English: If the original is in English, then for each unit of information in it, there are 1.22 $u$ in the German;[31] but if the original is in German, and the English is a translation, then for each unit of information in the English text, there are only 1.07 $u$ in German. Thus, the relation of the two texts, with respect to quantity of information, depends on the direction of the translation. We can assume that every process of translation leads to a relative lengthening of the text, since even the text content does not remain the same in translation. Because it is impossible to convey the text content exactly through the medium of another language, every translation becomes in part an explanation. Accordingly, a decided increase in information occurs. If we assume that in translating from English to German and back again, the increase in information remains the same, then we

---

[31] The quantity of information in a text was determined with the aid of formula (3): $H^m = mH_1$, where $m$ is the number of letters in a text (i.e., assuming that the letters are statistically independent). $H_1$ are quite insignificantly different for English and German (from the authors' data, $H_1$ for English is 4.08, and for German, it is 4.07). More accurate approximations to the amount of information per letter will apparently be more indicative, because for German and English, they differ to a much higher degree.

can determine both the value of this increase and the semantic weight of a unit of information in these languages as independent of the direction of translation: Let $x$ $u$ of German stand for 1 $u$ of information in English (then per 1 $u$ of German we have $1/x$ in English); furthermore, let the increase in information during translation be, for each unit of information of the initial text, $y$ $u$. Then, one can construct the following system of equations:

$$x + y = 1.22, \qquad 1.07 \left( \frac{1}{x} + y \right) = 1.00,$$

whence $x \sim 1.15$; $y \sim 0.06$.

Although the data obtained are not final, research in the direction indicated is undoubtedly most interesting. It would be very important to determine the values of both variables, as well as the semantic weight of a unit of information and the proportional increase in information in translation. Obviously, it would also be desirable to create conditions for determining these values individually. Thus, one can believe that scientific texts containing strictly defined terminology, such as mathematical texts, allow a maximum adequacy of translation, i.e., translation causes a minimal addition of information. In translating such text, the main change in quantity of information will be caused by the statistical structures of the codes involved. If we know how the amount of information changes in relation to the differences in the codes, we can then compare the growth of information for different texts or translators.

## 7.2. AMOUNT OF INFORMATION AND THE FUNCTIONAL LOAD OF PHONOLOGICAL CONTRASTS

The concepts of amount of information and redundancy as applied to language must not be thought of as completely new. Their value lies primarily in their close relation to other concepts, whose necessity was recognized by linguists long before attempts to use the methods of information theory in these areas appeared. There is an incontestable connection between the concepts of quantity of information and redundancy and the concept of functional load of phonemes or phonemic contrasts, the concept of strong and weak positions, and other phonological concepts. Bringing linguistic concepts closer to those of information theory can aid in making the former more precise.

The concept of the functional load of a phoneme and of phonological contrast is undoubtedly quite productive (see, for example, bibliography for Chapters I and II [7], p. 78). It is especially used in diachronic phonology, in which one of the main theses states that the probability of loss of a phonological contrast is inversely related to its functional load, since the loss of a contrast that plays a fundamental role in language has a negative influence on mutual comprehension. The concept of functional load is not exact enough. Functional load is usually connected with the number of minimal pairs containing a certain contrast (i.e., of pairs like *dom—tom, byl—pyl*, etc.), although such a method of evaluation is usually unsuccessful (see bibliography for Chapters I and II [7], pp. 79–83).

The possibilities of differentiation presented by a particular phonological system as a whole can be evaluated, for example, from the number of morphemes of a certain length that can be distinguished by the system. These possibilities are defined by the total number of phonemes, their frequencies, and the degree to which their mutual combinatory capabilities are restricted. Obviously, therefore, one can evaluate the differentiating possibilities of a phonological system from the amount of information per average phoneme in the system.

When phonological contrast is lost, two phonemes, or several pairs of phonemes, are merged into one, and the differentiating possibilities of the system decrease. For this reason, the difference $H - H^*$ (where $H$ is the amount of information per phoneme in the initial system, and $H^*$ is the amount of information in the system with one contrast lost) can be thought of as the differentiating load that falls on the particular contrast. It is clearly more appropriate to use the value $(H - H^*)/H$, which expresses the *fraction* of the functional load that falls on the contrast.

Such a method for evaluating functional load was proposed by Hockett,[32] who also asserted that the functional load so calculated for each individual contrast is so small that the loss of any

---

[32] See C. F. Hockett, *A Manual of Phonology*, Waverly Press, Baltimore, Maryland, 1955.

contrast can hardly reduce mutual comprehension. This assertion needs experimental verification.

## 7.3. A QUANTITATIVE EVALUATION OF POSITIONS IN PHONOLOGY AND SYNTAX

In studying the degree of use of phonological contrast in language, such concepts as that of the "position of maximum differentiation," "strong and weak positions," etc., are very important. Introduction of such concepts is related to the necessity of separating out rules that prevent the realization of certain phonemic distinctions (in Russian, for example, the position in an unstressed syllable is weak for vowels, because the number of contrasted vowels there decreases). However, the differentiation of only two forms of position—weak and strong—is clearly insufficient, since in many cases the actual picture is much more complex. Thus, in French there exists no position in which all ten non-nasalized vowels are distinguished. In a nonfinal syllable of a word, the contrast between open [ɛ] and closed [e] is neutralized: [ɛ] and [e] become positional variants in the pronunciation of most Frenchmen (as with *restons* [rɛstõ] and *laissons* [lesõ]); in the final and open syllable, contrast between [ø] and [œ] is neutralized, and between [o] and [ɔ], since [œ] and [ɔ] are impossible in the final position. Many neutralizations likewise occur before the so-called "lengthening" consonants [r], [z], [v], [z][33] in the final closed syllable.

It hardly seems useful to call any of these positions "strong," as opposed to "weak." It is not immediately clear which of these positions is the position of maximum differentiation. Nevertheless, quantitative comparison of positions among themselves can turn out to be quite essential in describing the phonological system. The positions can be compared by their degree of "weakness," which can be identified with redundancy per phoneme in certain conditions.

In linguistic description, the characteristics of position can vary: position before or after certain phonemes, position with

---

[33] [The [z] is repeated in the original text.—Tr.]

respect to stress, to end of word, etc. If we select one feature characterizing position—the position after a particular phoneme —then we can identify the differentiating possibilities of the phoneme in this position with its conditional entropy. For Russian, the conditional entropy of the first order is 3.82 $u$; since the maximum quantity of information with 42 phonemes is 5.38 $u$, the redundancy of 29 per cent can be considered a quantitative measure of the "weakness" of this position. There are no strong positions in this language, in that sense.

An evaluation of the differentiating possibilities of phonemes in structurally characterized positions would be interesting, e.g., a comparison of the amount of information in a phoneme located at the beginning or end of a word, after various classes of phonemes, etc.

In the area of syntax, several calculations have been made that now permit a quantitative comparison of the various syntactic positions in a sentence [12]. Research has been performed on English materials in which sentences written as strings of syntactic word classes were examined.[34] In a rather long text, all sentences eleven to twenty-five words in length were selected. The frequencies of various word classes in various positions in these sentences were calculated; the position was identified by the ordinal number of the word in the sentence. It was determined that in all positions, the frequencies of various word classes practically correspond with their over-all frequencies in the text. The first and last positions, for which there is a very large difference from the total frequency, are exceptional. Such a result is entirely natural: Only in those positions are structural restrictions imposed on the syntactic classes; thus, a sentence cannot end with an auxiliary, and hardly ever begins with a verb—the imperative is rarely found in written text—etc. The redundancy in each position was calculated from the frequencies obtained. Redundancy in English sentences is, on the average, about three times greater in the first and last positions than in the other positions, and it is somewhat greater in the final position than in the initial.

---

[34] Fries' simplified classification was used (see C. Fries, *The Structure of English*, Harcourt, Brace & Co., Inc., New York, 1952). Words were divided into five classes: noun, adjective, verb, adverb, and auxiliary.

## 7.4. Entropy and the Determination of Boundaries between Linguistic Units in Text

Attempts to apply the concept of entropy to the definition of boundaries between text elements deserve attention, especially those attempts to define the boundaries between elements of a higher level in a text that is described as a sequence of units of a lower level (e.g., the boundaries between morphemes or words in a sequence of phonemes). The first steps in this direction were taken in properly linguistic terms and were not immediately connected with a statistical approach to language.[35] Harris, for example, described the following procedure for text analysis. An utterance is taken, for example: "He is clever," transcribed phonologically as [hiyzklever]. All possible sentences beginning with the phoneme [h] are selected. The sentences can be drawn from a sufficiently large text or simply invented. A count is made of the number of phonemes that can follow this particular phoneme; they are called "descendants" of that phoneme. The number of descendants of the phoneme [h], according to the calculations of the author, is nine. Then, sentences beginning with the same two phonemes as the example sentence, i.e., with the combination [hi], are selected in an analogous fashion. At various points in the utterance, the number of descendants changes periodically—it falls, then rises, forms a peak, falls again, etc. Only strictly limited phoneme combinations are possible within a morpheme, although the following morpheme can begin with almost any phoneme. Thus, one can assume that a phoneme whose descendants form a peak is the last phoneme in a morpheme and, therefore, that the procedure described yields the splitting of text into morphemes. For the example given, the distribution of descendants is as follows:

| h | i | y | z | k | l | e | v | e | r |
|---|----|----|----|----|---|---|---|---|---|
| 9 | 14 | 29 | 29 | 11 | 7 | — | — | — | — |

[35] See Z. S. Harris, "From Phoneme to Morpheme," *Language*, Vol. 31, No. 2, 1955, pp. 190–222; see also S. Chatman, "Immediate Constituents and Expansion Analysis," *Word*, Vol. 11, No. 3, 1955, pp. 377–391.

The number of descendants attains a maximum after [hiy] and [hiyz], which corresponds with the real boundary between the morphemes in this sentence.

It is evident that calculation of the number of descendants amounts to an attempt to find a numerical expression for the indefiniteness of the following phoneme at a given point in the utterance, and information theory proposes to call this indefiniteness entropy. The possibilities of relating the boundaries of words or morphemes to peaks in entropy have been considered in a sequence of phonemes.[36] Suppose we have the sentence: "Let me in," transcribed as: [lɛt mi in]. The value $H_{a_1}$ is determined for each phoneme (see formula (4), p. 129). At first, $a_1$ is the phoneme [l], then the combination [lɛ], etc. (The author does not state positively that the calculated value is really not the entropy or the conditional entropy used by information theory—in particular, the quantity $H_{a_1}$—but, rather, that it is the amount of information under a fixed condition. The calculation of entropy or conditional entropy, i.e., the quantity $H_1$, would not lead to any useful results for our problem: $H_1$ is the same at all points in the utterance, and the conditional entropy decreases regularly as $n$ increases; see Figure 8.)

For our example, the values of $H_{a_1}$ are as follows:

| l | ε | t | m | i | i | n |
|------|------|------|------|------|------|------|
| .81 | .36 | .55 | .15 | .84 | .22 | — |

(Each phoneme is given a subscript corresponding to $H_{a_1}$, i.e., the indefiniteness of the following phoneme.) The growth of $H_{a_1}$ after [lɛt] and [lɛtmi] corresponds to the boundaries between morphemes in this sentence. This method was verified for 100 sentences and, from the author's calculations, gave positive results in about 85 per cent of the cases.

However, one cannot consider this direction of research productive. One of the reasons for lack of success in attempts to

---

[36] See C. S. Chomsky, "The Determination of Word Boundaries in Phonemic Sequences," *Collection of Papers Presented at the Seminar in Mathematical Linguistics,* Harvard University, Cambridge, Massachusetts, 1955 (mimeographed).

define boundaries between elements as points of increase in entropy is connected with the complexity of the language code, i.e., with the presence of several levels in it. Certain restrictions are imposed on text written as a sequence of phonemes; these limitations are connected with the presence not only of morphological, but also of syllabic and syntactic, structures in language. Therefore, in attempting to relate the entropy peak to morpheme boundaries, there arise, on the one hand, excess peaks corresponding to syllable boundaries, where, on the other hand, there cannot be peaks at the morpheme boundaries, since morpheme combinability is limited at the syntactic level (e.g., in the sentence *It kills me,* there will not be a peak after [itkil], since only the morphemes *-s* and *-ed* are possible after the morpheme *kill-,* according to the given syntactic conditions).

We note in addition that experiments can only be performed on very short sentences, since precision in the condition—i.e., lengthening of $a_1$—is connected with a decrease in $H_{a_1}$, and the tendency toward the latter's periodic growth at the boundaries of linguistic units disappears against this background. The main argument against this approach to defining the boundaries between language units is that probabilistic methods can only give the most probable boundaries, whereas the pieces of text having the "highest probability of being linguistic units" are hardly of interest to linguists. For example, if we analyzed not the sentence used as an example but one beginning with the word *letters,* we would obtain the fragment [lɛt], to which nothing corresponds on the level of content, and which is consequently not the unit we are seeking.

## 7.5. Redundancy, Interference, and the Problem of Ideality

Consciousness of the high degree of redundancy in language code apparently forces us to reëxamine several problems of phonology. Until recently, phonology clearly did not adequately account for the observation that sound distinctions fulfill a differentiating function only when they are sufficiently distinct to the listener's ear. In evaluating the differentiating capabilities of phonemes, one usually begins with a description of the articulation of the sounds and not with the actual capacity of the hearer to perceive them as different signals.[37] Several studies have shown that articulation differences between letters frequently do not function as an ideal guarantee of their always being distinguished by the hearer. For example, it has been established[38] that the distinctiveness of the phonemes [p], [t], and [k] in the final position of a word in English is considerably less than 100 per cent[39] (the experiments were conducted in ideal conditions of audibility; however, the listeners could not see the speaker's lip movements). Also of interest are data on the imperfect distinguishability of English vowel phonemes.[40]

If the probability of distortion of an individual signal is high enough even under ideal conditions of audibility, then it increases in the "average" situation of communication, and in some instances, it rises quite significantly.

Proper relation of each sound with a phoneme is not hindered by "external" circumstances alone (noise in the environment, narrowing of the frequency band, and other static in the transmitting apparatus). Great distortions are caused, for example, when the rate of speech increases; the sentence *Aleksandr Aleksandrovich vchera byl v teatre* [Alexander Alexandrovitch was at the theater yesterday] might sound like something transcribable as [sænsánčrəb″lt²atr²].[41] Likewise, a constant source of distortion of individual signals is the imperfect correspondence of the phonetic codes of speaker and listener caused, for example, by differences in dialect. Thus, in a real situation of language communication, not every bit of speech corresponds to a phoneme. Because of the redundancy of language, however,

---

[37] See H. Mol and E. M. Uhlenbeck, "Hearing and the Concept of Phoneme," *Lingua*, Vol. 8, No. 2, 1959, pp. 161–185.

[38] See F. W. Householder, "Unreleased *p, t, k,* in American English," in *For Roman Jakobson*, Mouton & Co., 's-Gravenhage, The Netherlands, 1956, pp. 235–248.

[39] Distinctiveness is evaluated with the aid of tables of meaningless words; regarding this, see, for example, L. R. Zinder, "Russkie artikulyatsionnye tablitsy" [Tables of Russian Articulation], *Trudy voennoj akademii im. S. M. Budennogo*, Collection 29–30, Leningrad, 1951, pp. 35–40.

[40] See H. L. Barney and H. K. Dunn, "Speech Analysis," in *Manual of Phonetics*, Kaisir, ed., North-Holland Publishing Co., Amsterdam, 1957. See also G. A. Miller and P. Nicely, "An Analysis of Perceptual Confusions Among Some English Consonants," *Journal of the Acoustical Society of America*, Vol. 27, No. 2, 1955, pp. 338–352.

[41] [In transliteration, ² stands for palatalization, ' for ь , and ″ for ъ .—Tr.]

to distinguish—i.e., "comprehend"—a word or sentence upon hearing it, it is not at all necessary to perceive every one of its phonemes precisely; the presence of syntactic bonds among phonemes permits a loss of some phonemic oppositions without a loss of comprehensibility, just as the multivalence or even homonymity of individual words does not, as a rule, hinder comprehension of the sense of the sentence as a whole, because of the presence of bonds among the words. Redundancy can be represented as that part of information which is already known to the hearer if he knows the statistical regularities of the particular code. The worse the auditory conditions, the greater the role played, relatively speaking, by redundancy information during perception.

In order to get some idea of the kind of role that redundancy plays in speech comprehension, we shall consider a situation in which redundancy decreases significantly and the main load is taken up by the differentiating capacities of the phonemes. An example of such a situation is presented by R. O. Jakobson and M. Halle [27]; under some particular circumstances, the listener is told the last names of people with whom he is not acquainted, or other proper nouns he does not know. In this case, unlike others, neither the speech context nor that of the situation can aid him in comprehending the message: The proper names are not found in the listener's vocabulary; moreover, in last names and proper nouns, the laws of phoneme combinability are often broken (as in the names Przewalsky, Bkhilai, etc.[42]). In this instance, the average redundancy per phoneme is much less than the average level characteristic for the language as a whole. As a result, the idealization that can safeguard a language in such a situation is clearly insufficient. (For example, in the course of a person's education, proper nouns are written on the board; otherwise, a hearer would have only a very approximate idea of their phonology.)

If the statistical bonds among phonemes play such a great role in speech comprehension "at the phonemic level," then speech is not perceived "phonemically" (hence the lack of success in attempts to construct machines for describing oral

---

[42] [Of course, the author of this chapter is speaking here from the point of view of the Great Russian phonetic system.—Tr.]

speech[43]). If language were perceived phoneme-by-phoneme, then the correct transmission of information via language would be impossible. In fact, a very complex process of "decoding" takes place during the perception of a language message: During decoding "at the phoneme level," certain signals can be incorrectly comprehended; but since a word is only a small part of combinations of signals, even a small group of undistorted signals can permit correction of the error most of the time. It may even be true that there will not be enough of these correctly received signals to correct the error, and the entire word will be mistaken. But combinations of words are not arbitrary; thus, the error can be corrected at a higher level. For just this reason, a language message is not comprehended immediately after the next sound has been pronounced, but somewhat hesitantly (for some experimental data on this matter, see [7]).

More complexity in the coding system is apparently the main way to optimize technical communication. These systems will thus be models of the process by which human beings communicate using language.[44]

## 8. *The Tendency toward Optimality in Language Codes*

Up to now, we have spoken only of the bonds among units on the same level. It is also of interest to note the relation among units of this and a higher level, i.e., the means of constructing larger units from elementary symbols.

We have explained that language is distinguished by a great deal of redundancy that is the consequence of its "structuredness" and that guarantees its close approach to the ideal. Even more interesting are tendencies of an oppositional character in other aspects of language, namely, in the formation of larger units from small ones; here, language proves to be highly effective and, at least in some respects, close to the optimal code.

We shall note the latter characteristic at the level of the rela-

---

[43] For example, see D. G. Fry and P. Denes, "Experiments in Mechanical Speech Recognition," in *Information Theory*, C. Cherry, ed., Academic Press Inc., New York, 1956, pp. 206–212.

[44] See R. M. Fano, "The Challenge of Digital Communication," *IRE Transactions on Information Theory*, Vol. IT-4, No. 2, June, 1958, pp. 63–64.

tionship between distinctive features and phonemes, and also at the level of the relationship between letters and words.

Data on this matter (for Russian) are contained in C. Cherry, M. Halle, and R. O. Jakobson's work [18]. The total number of distinctive features taking part in the differentiation of Russian phonemes is 11 (see [18]). Each phoneme can be unambiguously characterized by means of such features as "voicedness" and "vowel quality." In general, one can distinguish $2^{11} =$ 2,048 phonemes, using the 11 features, and, consequently, the total number of distinctive features is much larger than the minimum necessary for distinguishing Russian phonemes from one another. However, not all features participate in the identification of each phoneme, but only of some of them; thus, the feature of "voicedness" is not distinctive for the phoneme [č]: Although the phoneme [č] is unvoiced, phonetically speaking, still the corresponding voiced sound (encountered, for example, at the end of the word *szhech'* in the combination *szhech' by*) is not an independent phoneme in Russian; therefore, the "voicedness" of [č] has no differentiating function; the feature of "nasalization" is distinctive for only a very small number of phonemes, since there are no nasal vowels in Russian nor any sound like [ŋ], etc. Therefore, one can construct the following model of a phoneme: Phonemes are coded with strings of distinctive features; all of these are binary, i.e., they can take the values 0 or 1 (e.g., the values of the feature of "voicedness" are as follows: voiced—1, unvoiced—0). The number of symbols in the string is variable; e.g., in identifying the phoneme [a] four features are relevant, while nine apply to the phoneme [t] (see Table 3, p. 150). Phonemes occur in speech with unequal frequencies; therefore, the "coding" of phonemes by distinctive features will be optimized if the shortest code combinations are written for the most frequent phonemes, and, conversely, the longest for the least frequent. The degree of approximation of the phoneme code to the optimum can be evaluated by the degree to which the average number of distinctive features per phoneme occurring in text approaches the amount of information in the phoneme (we have in mind the value $H_1$). The average number of distinctive features per phoneme occurring in text, according to Cherry *et al.*, is 5.79, while $H_1$ for Russian is 4.78; as we see, the divergence of the real figure from the optimum is not so very great.

It is not hard to comprehend that this statistical regularity is the result of very simple facts.[45] The total number of vowels in the Russian phonological system, as in many other systems, is much lower than the number of consonants. Therefore, the feature of vowel versus consonant divides all phonemes into two unequal groups: Among the vowels, the number of phonemes is considerably less than it is among the consonants. Hence, the number of features needed to identify a vowel phoneme is less than the number needed for a consonant. Since there must be a vowel in every syllable, the relative frequency of vowels is, on the average, higher than that for consonants. Thus, the relatively large frequency and small number of differentiating features for vowels is a main source of optimality of the phoneme code.

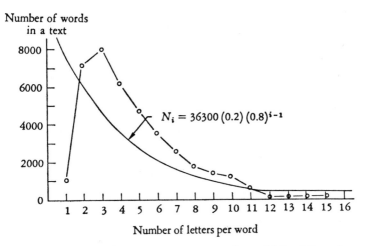

FIGURE 10. Word Frequency as a Function of Word Length.

On the subject of the relation between word length and word frequency, Miller *et al.* obtained interesting data ([33], [34]). The research was performed on English-language materials. The results are shown in Figure 10, where word frequency is presented as a function of word length (counts were made on a text

---

[45] On this matter, see N. Chomsky's review of R. O. Jakobson and M. Halle's "Fundamentals of Language," in *International Journal of American Linguistics*, Vol. 23, No. 3, 1957, pp. 234–241.

36,300 words in length). The experimental curve rather closely approaches the curve of inverse proportionality. This kind of distribution of the letters in words makes the average length of a word in text minimal and brings the amount of information per average letter closer to the maximum. Thus, word coding with letters is nearly optimal.

This phenomenon was noted some time ago (see bibliography for Chapter V, [49]), and many attempts have been made to give some reasonable explanation for it. The simplest explanation has been proposed by Miller and Newman [33]. Let us assume that words originate by a probabilistic process—say, by a Markov process. The test consists of finding whether a letter or space occurs. The probability of a space in English is about 0.2, while the probability of a letter is 0.8. Thus, the process of creating a word can be represented as in the scheme in Figure 11.[46]

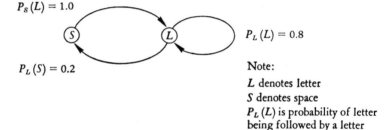

$P_S(L) = 1.0$

$P_L(L) = 0.8$

$P_L(S) = 0.2$

Note:

L denotes letter
S denotes space
$P_L(L)$ is probability of letter being followed by a letter

FIGURE 11.   Scheme for the Process of Word Creation.

The probability of creating a concrete word $i$ letters in length by such a process is determined by the two following facts: (a) the number of different chains of letters increases with increase in the length of the chain; (b) the probability of creation of a chain of corresponding length decreases with increase in the length of the chain. Actually, the probability of creating a chain $i$ letters long is $(0.2)(0.8)^{i-1}$, and consequently the shorter the chain is, the greater the probability. A result of these two facts is the inverse dependency between the frequency of a word and the number of letters contained in it. Thus, the optimum relation between word frequency and word length emerges as a nec-

---

[46] [The numbers in the diagram make the probability of a space about 0.167, not 0.2.—Tr.]

essary consequence, if one assumes that words are created by a random process of the type already described; in other words, this relation is the result of the fact that a shift in the location of the space in a text is accidental. In fact, as Miller has shown, an analogous relation between length and probability for a "word" obtains if the "word" is defined as an interval between two occurrences of the letter *e* in English text (or rather, the dependency holds up even more perfectly in this case).

Miller's important results are as follows. It turns out that the optimum relation between a word's text frequency and its length is primarily due to auxiliaries. If two graphs are constructed, one showing the relationship between word frequency and word length for auxiliaries and one for full-meaning words,[47] then the approach to inverse proportionality will be better for auxiliaries than it is for all words taken as a whole, while for full-meaning words, frequency and length are almost independent. There is as yet no meaningful explanation of this fact.

## 9. Limits on the Possible Applications of Information Theory to Language

To summarize, regarding the possibilities of applying information theory to linguistic problems, one can only say the following: Because of the peculiarities of mathematical information theory, only the formal or, more precisely speaking, the code aspects of language can be studied by its methods. Therefore, the greatest value of information theory lies in its application to the study of phonological and "letter" aspects of language. Also, these aspects are the most suitable for application of the ideas of information theory, because any model representing

---

[47] The criteria existing in linguistics for distinguishing auxiliaries from full-meaning words are recognized by the authors to be inexact, and a complete list of the words considered auxiliary for the purpose of the counts is presented in their work. Several of these words cannot help but elicit surprise. We note, for example, that complex numerals such as *twenty-seven* are considered auxiliaries and are written without the space. The authors assert, however, that their choice was not all based on such considerations as the lengths or frequencies of words.

the process of creation of a message as the "emission" of one symbol after another in a linear sequence, for all levels of language besides the two indicated above, is not very productive[48] (take, for example, the complex hierarchical structure of a sentence at the syntactic level).

It may be that R. Carnap and Y. Bar-Hillel's semantic information theory ([13], [14], [22]) can play a large role in future studies of the semantic aspect of language. This theory is based on R. Carnap's concept of inductive probability, and it develops several special questions in logical semantics. The theory considers semantic questions in artificial languages constructed for the purpose of describing a narrowly limited situation for which one can enumerate all the objects, their possible properties, and the logical bonds among elementary assertions about the properties of the objects. It may be that semantic information theory can be used for future study of natural languages, at least within limited spheres of their application.

## BIBLIOGRAPHY FOR CHAPTER VI

1. Brillyuen, L., *Nauka i teoriya informatsiya* [*Science and Information Theory*], Fizmatgiz, Moscow, 1960.
2. Goldman, S., *Teoriya informatsii* [*Information Theory*], Prentice-Hall, Inc., New York, 1953; Izd-vo inostr. lit., Moscow, 1957.
3. Lebedev, D. S., and V. A. Garmash, "O vozmozhnosti uvelicheniya skorosti peredachi telegrafnykh soobshchenii" ["Possibility of Increasing the Transmission Speed in Telegraphic Communications"], *Elektrosvyaz'*, No. 1, 1958, pp. 68–69.
4. ———, and ———, "Statisticheskij analiz trekhbukvennykh sochetanij russkogo teksta" ["Statistical Analysis of Three-Letter Combinations in Russian Text"], *Problemy peredachi informatsii*, Vol. 2, 1959, pp. 78–80. (Translated: JPRS 3598, U.S. Joint Publications Research Service, August, 1960, pp. 31–35.)
5. Poletaev, I. A., *Signal; o nekotorykh ponyatiyakh kibernetiki*

---

[48] See N. Chomsky, *Syntactic Structures*, Mouton & Co., 's-Gravenhage, The Netherlands, 1956, regarding the inadequacy of the Markov process as a model for the grammar of a natural language.

[*Signals; Some Cybernetic Concepts*], Izd-vo "Sovetskoe radio," Moscow, 1958, 403 pp.

6. Kharkevich, A. A., *Ocherki obshchej teorii svyazi* [*Outline of a General Theory of Communications*], Gostekhizdat, Moscow, 1955, 268 pp.

7. Chistovich, L. A., V. V. Alyakrinsky, and V. A. Abulyan, "Vremennye zaderzhki pri povtorenii slyshimoj rechi" ["Occasional Hesitations in the Repetition of Audible Speech"], *Voprosy psikhologii,* No. 1, January-February, 1960, pp. 114–120.

8. Ashby, W. R., *Vvedenie v kibernetiku* [*An Introduction to Cybernetics*], Chapman & Hall, Ltd., London, 1956; Izd-vo inostr. lit., Moscow, 1959.

9. Yaglom, A. M., "Primenenie idej teorii informatsii k opredeleniyu vremeni psikhologicheskikh reaktsij" ["Application of the Ideas of Information Theory To Determine the Time of Psychological Reactions"], *Matematicheskoe prosveshchenie,* No. 5, 1960, pp. 246–252.

10. Yaglom, I. M., R. L. Dobrushin, and A. M. Yaglom, "Yazyk i teoriya informatsii" ["Information Theory and Linguistics"], *Voprosy yazykoznaniya,* No. 1, 1960, pp. 100–110. (Translated: JPRS 3796, U.S. Joint Publications Research Service, Series "K": *Soviet Developments in Information Processing and Machine Translation,* September, 1960, pp. 12–31.)

11. Yaglom, A. M., and I. M. Yaglom, *Veroyatnost' i informatsiya* [*Probability and Information*], 2nd edition, 1960; originally *Wahrscheinlichkeit und Information,* VEB Deutscher Verlag der Wissenschaften, Berlin, 1960.

12. Aborn, M., and H. Rubenstein, "Word Class Distribution in Sentences of Fixed Length," *Language,* Vol. 32, No. 4, Part 1, 1956, pp. 666–674.

13. Bar-Hillel, Y., "An Examination of Information Theory," *Philosophy of Science,* Vol. 22, No. 2, 1955, pp. 86–105.

14. ———, and R. Carnap, "Semantic Information," *British Journal for the Philosophy of Science,* Vol. 4, 1953–1954, pp. 147–157.

15. Barnard, G. A., "Statistical Calculation of Word Entropies for Four Western Languages," *IRE Transactions on Information Theory,* Vol. IT-1, No. 1, March, 1955, pp. 49–53.

16. Burton, N. G., and J. C. R. Licklider, "Long-Range Constraints in Statistical Structure of Printed English," *American Journal of Psychology,* Vol. 68, No. 4, 1955, pp. 650–653.

17.  Cherry, C., *On Human Communication,* John Wiley & Sons, Inc., New York, 1957.
18.  ———, M. Halle, and R. O. Jakobson, "Towards the Logical Description of Languages in Their Phonemic Aspect," *Language,* Vol. 29, No. 1, 1953, pp. 34–46.
19.  Chomsky, N., "Review of V. Belevitch's 'Langage des machines et langage humain,'" *Language,* Vol. 34, No. 2, Part 1, 1958, pp. 99–105.
20.  ———, and G. A. Miller, "Finite State Languages," *Information and Control,* Vol. 1, No. 1, 1958, pp. 91–112.
21.  Dewey, G., *Relative Frequency of English Speech Sounds,* Harvard University Press, Cambridge, Massachusetts, 1923.
22.  Elias, P., "Review of R. Carnap and Y. Bar-Hillel's 'An Outline of a Theory of Semantic Information,'" *Journal of Symbolic Logic,* Vol. 19, No. 3, September, 1954, pp. 230–232.
23.  Frick, F. C., and W. H. Sumby, "Control Tower Language," *Journal of the Acoustical Society of America,* Vol. 24, No. 6, 1952, pp. 595–596.
24.  Fritz, E. L., and G. W. Grier, "Pragmatic Communication," in H. Quastler, ed., *Information Theory in Psychology,* The Free Press, Glencoe, Illinois, 1956, pp. 252–254.
25.  Fry, D. G., "Communication Theory and Linguistic Theory," *IRE Transactions on Information Theory,* Vol. IT-1, 1954.
26.  Hockett, C. F., "Review of C. E. Shannon and W. Weaver's 'The Mathematical Theory of Communication,'" *Language,* Vol. 29, No. 1, 1953, pp. 69–93.
27.  Jakobson, R. O., and M. Halle, *Fundamentals of Language,* Mouton & Co., 's-Gravenhage, The Netherlands, 1956.
28.  Küpfmüller, K., "Die Entropie der Deutschen Sprache" ["Entropy of the German Language"], *Fernmeldetechnische Zeitschrift [For Machine Science],* Hf. 6, 1954.
29.  Lees, R. B., "Review of L. Apostel, B. Mandelbrot, and A. Morf's 'Logique, langage et théorie de l'information,'" *Language,* Vol. 35, No. 2, Part 1, 1959, pp. 271–303.
30.  Miller, G. A., *Language and Communication,* McGraw-Hill Book Co., Inc., New York, 1951.
31.  ———, "Information Theory and the Study of Speech," in *Current Trends in Information Theory,* University of Pittsburgh Press, Pittsburgh, Pennsylvania, 1953–1954, pp. 119–139.
32.  ———, G. A. Heise, and W. Lichten, "The Intelligibility of Speech as a Function of the Context of Test Materials,"

*Journal of Experimental Psychology,* Vol. 41, 1951, pp. 329–335.

33. Miller, G. A., and E. B. Newman, "Tests of a Statistical Explanation of the Rank-Frequency Relation for Words in Written English," *American Journal of Psychology,* Vol. 71, No. 1, 1958, p. 209.

34. ———, ———, and E. A. Friedman, "Length-Frequency Statistics for Written English," *Information and Control,* Vol. 1, No. 4, 1958, pp. 370–389.

35. Newman, E. B., and L. J. Gerstman, "A New Method for Analyzing Printed English," *Journal of Experimental Psychology,* Vol. 44, 1952, pp. 114–125.

36. Pratt, F., *Secret and Urgent: The Story of Codes and Ciphers,* The Bobbs-Merrill Co., Inc., Indianapolis, Indiana, c. 1939.

37. Shannon, C. E., "A Mathematical Theory of Communication," *Bell System Technical Journal,* Vol. 27, No. 3, 1948, pp. 379–423; Vol. 27, No. 4, 1948, pp. 623–656.

38. ———, "Prediction and Entropy of Printed English," *Bell System Technical Journal,* Vol. 30, January, 1951, pp. 50–64.

39. ———, "Redundancy of English," in *Cybernetics: Transactions of the Eighth Conference,* New York, 1951, pp. 123–158.

40. ———, and W. W. Weaver, *The Mathematical Theory of Communication,* University of Illinois Press, Urbana, Illinois, 1949.

41. "Proceedings of the Speech Communication Conference at M.I.T.," *Journal of the Acoustical Society of America,* Vol. 22, No. 6, 1950; Vol. 24, No. 6, 1952.

# INDEX

# SELECTED RAND BOOKS

Baker, C. L., and F. J. Gruenberger. *The First Six Million Prime Numbers*. Madison, Wis.: The Microcard Foundation, 1959.

Bellman, Richard. *Adaptive Control Processes: A Guided Tour*. Princeton, N.J.: Princeton University Press, 1961.

Bellman, Richard. *Dynamic Programming*. Princeton, N.J.: Princeton University Press, 1957.

Bellman, Richard. *Introduction to Matrix Analysis*. New York: McGraw-Hill Book Company, Inc., 1960.

Bellman, Richard (ed.). *Mathematical Optimization Techniques*. Berkeley and Los Angeles: University of California Press, 1963.

Bellman, Richard, and Kenneth L. Cooke. *Differential-Difference Equations*. New York: Academic Press, 1963.

Bellman, Richard, and Stuart E. Dreyfus. *Applied Dynamic Programming*. Princeton, N.J.: Princeton University Press, 1962.

Buchheim, Robert W., and the Staff of The RAND Corporation. *Space Handbook: Astronautics and Its Applications*. New York: Random House, Inc., 1959.

Dorfman, Robert, Paul A. Samuelson, and Robert M. Solow. *Linear Programming and Economic Analysis*. New York: McGraw-Hill Book Company, Inc., 1958.

Dresher, Melvin. *Games of Strategy: Theory and Applications*. Englewood Cliffs, N.J.: Prentice-Hall, Inc., 1961.

Dubyago, A. D. *The Determination of Orbits*. Translated from the Russian by R. D. Burke, G. Gordon, L. N. Rowell, and F. T. Smith. New York: The Macmillan Company, 1961.

Edelen, Dominic G. B. *The Structure of Field Space: An Axiomatic Formulation of Field Physics.* Berkeley and Los Angeles: University of California Press, 1962.

Ford, L. R., Jr., and D. R. Fulkerson. *Flows in Networks.* Princeton, N.J.: Princeton University Press, 1962.

Gale, David. *The Theory of Linear Economic Models.* New York: McGraw-Hill Book Company, Inc., 1960.

Gruenberger, F. J., and D. D. McCracken. *Introduction to Electronic Computers.* New York: John Wiley & Sons, Inc., 1963.

Hastings, Cecil, Jr. *Approximations for Digital Computers.* Princeton, N.J.: Princeton University Press, 1955.

Markowitz, H. M., B. Hausner, and H. W. Karr. *SIMSCRIPT: A Simulation Programming Language.* Englewood Cliffs, N.J.: Prentice-Hall, Inc., 1963.

McKinsey, J. C. C. *Introduction to the Theory of Games.* New York: McGraw-Hill Book Company, Inc., 1952.

Newell, Allen (ed.). *Information Processing Language-V Manual.* Englewood Cliffs, N.J.: Prentice-Hall, Inc., 1961.

The RAND Corporation. *A Million Random Digits with 100,000 Normal Deviates.* Glencoe, Ill.: The Free Press, 1955.

Williams, J. D. *The Compleat Strategyst: Being a Primer on the Theory of Games of Strategy.* New York: McGraw-Hill Book Company, Inc., 1954.